PROJECT MEASUREMENT

The books in the Project Management Essential Library series provide project managers with new skills and innovative approaches to the fundamentals of effectively managing projects.

Additional titles in the series include:

Managing Projects for Value, John C. Goodpasture

Effective Work Breakdown Structures, Gregory T. Haugan

Project Planning and Scheduling, Gregory T. Haugan

Managing Project Quality, Timothy J. Kloppenborg and Joseph A. Petrick

Project Estimating and Cost Management, Parviz F. Rad

Project Risk Management: A Proactive Approach, Paul S. Royer

MANAGEMENTCONCEPTS

www.managementconcepts.com

PROJECT MEASUREMENT

Steve Neuendorf

MANAGEMENTCONCEPTS

Vienna, Virginia

(((
MANAGEMENTCONCEPTS

8230 Leesburg Pike, Suite 800
Vienna, VA 22182
(703) 790-9595
Fax: (703) 790-1371
www.managementconcepts.com

Printed in the United States of America

Library of Congress Cataloging-in-Publication Data

Neuendorf, Steve, 1951–
    Project measurement / Steve Neuendorf
        p. cm. — (Project management essential library)
    Includes bibliographical references and index.
    ISBN 1-56726-140-X
    1. Project management. 2. Industrial management. I. Title. II. Series.
T56.8 .N48 2001
658.5—dc21

                                    2001044562

About the Author

Steve Neuendorf has more than 25 years of consulting, management, industrial engineering, and measurement experience, including 15 years directly related to management, measurement, and improvement of software engineering projects and processes. Steve also has extensive management consulting experience. He has a BA and an MBA from the University of Puget Sound with post-graduate work in information management, and a JD from Seattle University. Steve also has extensive teaching experience, ranging from academics to hands-on workshops.

*I Dedicate This Book
to My Wife Jeanie*

Table of Contents

Preface

roject Measurement is intended as a reference for project managers and anyone interested in implementing, improving, or evaluating a measurement program. It is organized so that Chapters 1, 2, and 3 should be common reading. The remaining chapters and subsections represent aspects of practical measurement that you may want to accomplish. With that consideration, many concepts are repeated throughout the book to avoid the need to refer to other sections that may not be of interest to you. If you are reading the book "cover to cover," it should be interesting to note that some variation in common materials captures the variation in reality. This book does not treat measurement as an academic subject with right and wrong answers. Measurement is a tool, and the greater the skill you develop at using the tool, the greater the likelihood that you will achieve the results you seek.

Quite a bit has been written about measurement, particularly as it relates to project management. What distinguishes this book from others is that it takes an outside view of the organization needing to implement measurement. This viewpoint should help readers have a better chance of succeeding in measurement. What does that really mean? The vast majority of measurement programs are designed from inside the organization. Existing data are the first default used to drive measurement. The overriding assumption is that those who understand how a process is done will also understand how to measure it and be able to identify meaningful improvements or innovations.

Project managers understand risk. Not having the right skills behind a process greatly increases the risk that the process will fail to produce the desired result or will produce the desired result using considerably more resources than were necessary or planned for.

Succeeding in measurement means that everyone who needs quantitative information has the information they need in time to support the organization in accomplishing its mission and achieving its goals. Of course, there are a few other success factors for measurement, including efficiency, no disruptions, security considerations, no waste, etc.; but if measurement does not accomplish the goal of everyone having the quantitative information they need, chalk it up as a failure. This book is intended to help you achieve success in measurement.

Much of what organizations do or want to do is dependent on the ability and capacity to assess actions and results quantitatively. Measurement is the *sine qua non* (essential element or condition) for success in key initiatives, that is, those vital to the continued success and viability of the organization: faster, better, cheaper.

Measurement is a separate discipline from what is being measured. Special knowledge and skills must be employed to realize the full potential of measurement. It is important to note the comparison between experience and education. Experience is the basis for knowing how to do something well in a particular way, while education teaches that there are different ways of doing something. Knowing a process or even understanding it so that you understand the impact of changes or can trace changes in results to their causes is not the same as knowing how to measure that process or to how to conceive and implement a measurement program that will meet the goals that inspired the measurement program in the first place. Similarly, being good at a particular skill or discipline does not ensure that one will be a good project manager for that skill or discipline.

Measurement fits into several classifications, ranging from an exacting scientific discipline to a simple task. For the pragmatic purposes of this book, measurement is viewed primarily as a communications tool, and the "stakeholders" are its customers and users. For measurement to be effective and to succeed, stakeholder requirements must be reflected in the structure and operation of the measurement program. Part of this book describes how to engage stakeholders in the measurement program design process.

Since measurement supports the evolution of the subject being measured, measurement must evolve also. If we expect rapid change, it is likely that the measurement that supports the change decisions and validates the change results must evolve at least as fast, if not faster, than the change itself.

Measurement has a definite lifecycle. A generic learning cycle (the Kirkpatrick Model, 1971[1]) applies to measurement where the discipline or process being examined is not measured and is not particularly effective, efficient, or robust. Sometimes it works very well, but in general, the process

---

[1]D.L. Kirkpatrick, *A Practical Guide for Supervisory Training and Development* (Reading MA: Addison-Wesley, 1971).

is not reliable at producing the desired results in all aspects in which it should be evaluated (*unconscious incompetence*).

The first step in the maturing process is to change the awareness of what goes on in the process through the measurement and use of quantitative tools. Once we are at least aware of the inadequacies and inefficiencies of the process, changes can be made to fix what does not work, add what is missing, and eliminate what is unnecessary (*conscious incompetence*). Measurement evolves with the changes until the process is mature and performs at a consistently high level of effectiveness and efficiency—generally known as robust (*conscious competence*). At the high end, where changes to the process are small and infrequent, the need for so much measurement decreases and the process evolves to the state of being efficient, effective, and robust without the need for measurement to confirm this state (*unconscious competence*).

As you progress, keep this sequence in mind. Chances are that you are not unconsciously competent, and initiating the measurement program will confirm it. In fact, many first measurement efforts fail because they succeed in illustrating incompetence that was not contemplated. It follows, then, that something must be wrong with the measurement—right?

This book provides considerable material intended to help you move from a state of unconscious incompetence to one of conscious incompetence. Some information to help you achieve conscious competence is also provided, but that evolution requires so much customization and flexibility that no effective prescriptive resource is available.

A NOTE ABOUT SECURITY

The best environment is an open environment where there are no secrets and there is no fear. Unfortunately, there are few real open environments in organizations. There is always an element of fear that data will be abused or used for purposes other than that for which it was intended. It seems that downsizing has become an unavoidable aspect of our business cycles. One fair and objective way to make the unpleasant task of selecting who will stay and who will go is to find data that illustrate a trait or condition that associates some putative business value with individuals. As a result, data are often prejudged in terms of their negative potential, just as risks are evaluated in project management in terms of the likelihood of abuse of the data—and the consequences. If the possibilities look too dangerous, the data are not collected, not communicated, or "massaged" to mitigate the risk of abuse at the cost of precluding their intended use or misrepresenting the reality that the data are intended to portray.

There is no way to accommodate fear in the organization. The commitment that makes a measurement program work has to include effective and absolute prohibitions against the abuse of data. Data that are past their usefulness should be destroyed. Data that are retained should be made anonymous or made accessible only to those whose responsibility includes protecting the data from abuse.

Steve Neuendorf

Acknowledgments

I would like to acknowledge the encouragement and support of the people at Management Concepts in making this book a reality.

CHAPTER 1

Why Measure?

There are some excellent reasons for not measuring. No one can say that you missed your goal; it is just another opinion. Cost savings are substantial, since measurement can be costly. It may be that you feel you are the best at what you do and have everything under control. Measurement would only confirm that, so why bother?

The truth is that everyone measures; everyone has some sort of quantification for what they do. In business, measurement is forced to be somewhat formal because of accounting requirements. For public companies, certain other standards are imposed that prescribe measurements and measurement discipline and formality. Throughout the organization, everyone has at least an informal mental picture of the quantitative nature of what is necessary to do his or her job and manage risks. A detailed report is unnecessary for the material people to know how many pallets are on the dock or for the production people to know the size of various queues or the inventory of key supplies and materials. In fact, it is an accepted generalization that during a relatively steady state, even the most comprehensive measurement program has little effect on current or future events.

However, the opportunity to effect change or the ability to respond efficiently to change is lost if there is little or no measurement formality or discipline. If a key person leaves, the successor must start from scratch to figure out what his or her predecessor knew and needed to know to perform that job. If there is a significant change in a product or the demand for a product, the adjustments needed are made by trial and error, which can be costly. Usually, any ad-hoc need for information is met with inappropriately high cost in gathering the information and a high risk that the information will be inaccurate or unverifiable.

Thus, chances are that even if an individual is convinced that he or she is not using measurement, the organization likely is measuring, quantifying, and supporting decisions in an informal manner. The change is not in going from not measuring to measuring, but in going from a lack of formality to more formality and from a lack of communication to a much higher level of communication regarding quantitative information.

SOME MYTHS AND FACTS ABOUT MEASUREMENT

When someone does not want to do something, it does not really matter why it isn't done as much as it matters that it isn't done. Since myths usually contradict or exaggerate facts, perpetuating a generally accepted myth can often be an effective means to prevent measurement from moving forward.

Myth: Measurement Is Expensive

Fact: Measurement is a cost. In a business, the concepts of expensive and cheap do not apply. Outlays have a cost—the amount of cash or other resources committed. Benefits are always associated with costs. Cost-benefit analyses are used to support decisions about which outlays should be made. For example, successful software engineering process measurement programs require an outlay of 1 percent to 3 percent of the total cost of software engineering. Many industry leaders invest more than 5 percent of total costs in measurement. Typical benefits realized by these companies as an indirect result are continuously increased product and service quality, as well as annual improvements in productivity of 10 percent to 15 percent.

Myth: Measurements Can Be Used against the Persons Being Measured

Fact: The myth is true, in the same sense that matches can be used to incinerate civilization. It is possible to say that they can be, but only once. After that, what is done is no longer measurement, but is more akin to creative writing and risk management. Dr. W. Edwards Deming observed that the system dictates its own performance; the performance of people working in the system is largely a product of the system. In a system fraught with fear, one compensates by producing measures that mitigate the results of what the people in the system fear. One of Deming's famous 14 points is to drive out fear.[1] Measurements are used correctly to assess the performance of the system and to identify system improvements.

Myth: Measuring Can Improve Processes

Fact: Processes can be improved only by changing the processes. Measurement helps identify beneficial changes that must be implemented for improvements to occur. However, processes can be changed independent of measurement. The advantage of measurement is leveraging the change investment. Good measurement identifies those changes with the highest return. For example, in software engineering, if processes are routinely changed by investing in all the newest tools and technologies, an annual improvement of about 3 percent in productivity can be realized. Most of what is acquired ends up as "shelfware" and considerable effort is spent trying out these new tools that are never used. By using measurements to identify the best improvements and focusing training on implementing those improvements, the same investment can consistently yield 10 percent to 15 percent productivity improvements.

DEMONSTRATING LEADERSHIP AND ARTICULATING STRATEGY

Another opportunity for a comprehensive corporate measurement effort is to demonstrate leadership. It is widely accepted that good leaders are those who inspire a clear vision of where the organization is headed. If the vision can be expressed quantitatively, where you are in relation to the vision and your progress toward the vision can also be expressed quantitatively. With direct feedback concerning progress, it is much easier to continue on a successful course or to change to an alternate course.

ENABLING MANAGEMENT

Empowered is one of those overused and abused words, but it is hard to talk about measurement and management without embracing the notion of empowerment. By empowering someone, power that was previously at a higher organizational level is now reassigned and redefines a person's role, giving him or her the responsibility for making a decision, authority to make that decision, and accountability for the results of that decision. In truth, most people are uncomfortable making decisions, and sociologists have noted that this discomfort is really at the root of our hierarchical social and economic system.

Measurement and quantitative information are essential parts of decision support systems (DSS). They are intended to increase the decision maker's confidence level by providing a better understanding of alternative options for a decision and for forecasting the consequences of any particular decision option.

Another consequence of empowering those at lower levels of an organization is that they will be within the larger population of the organization and will naturally have more communication channels to deal with. Decision makers at lower levels need to provide more people with certain information and, in turn, receive information from more people than was required when the decision was made at a higher level of the organization. Less of this information is summarized ("the bottom line") than is customary when conveying information to higher organizational levels.

EFFECTING PROCESS PROFICIENCY AND IMPROVEMENT

As noted in the Preface, the maturing process of going from unconsciousness to consciousness implies that measurement is not a goal. Rather, it is a means of achieving the goal of competence, however that might be expressed. This relationship is also important to consider when the organization is looking to cut costs. If cutting costs merely meant spending less money, it would not matter what was cut. However, what it really means is that costs need to be cut by something less than the impact of those cost cuts on revenues.

A good analogy would be to liken cost cutting to a surgical operation. If the goal is to cut out waste and the first thing identified as waste is the lighting in the operating room, there cannot be much hope for successful surgery. In fact, not only is the patient (*process*) in grave danger because the operation will be performed in darkness, but there is also a risk to the surgical team (*unintended staff loss*). While this analogy sounds ridiculous, it is the equivalent of organizations embarking on cost cutting by eliminating or substantially reducing measurement and other activities aimed at improving processes, which almost always results in faster, better, and cheaper performance.

ALIGNING THE FACETS

Serious improvement involves much more than improving processes. Organizations are multifaceted organisms (as the name implies) and many factors must come together for success. Similar to the marathon runner who is in excellent condition except for a foot blister, although everything else is perfect, that one weak area may result in an unsuccessful outcome. Organizational facets, too, can be clearly identified. For example, consider an organization with the major facets of leadership, strategy, project management, the management of project management, process, and environment. It is easy to see how, for example, the best processes will not excel if project management is poor, or how a poor strategy will not succeed even if all other facets are at their best. Usually, these relationships are the overlooked correct answers to questions arising from the lack of results after significant investments in one or more facets. A fortune can be spent on process; however, if the environment in which that process is expected to perform is not aligned properly, the process will not perform as expected.

An effective measurement program identifies all necessary facets for success and works toward evaluating the alignment of these facets. This point is significant in establishing expectations for improvement activity, both in estimating the investment to achieve success and in understanding the results from such investment.

Measurement is important, but deceptively simple-looking; a misguided venture into measurement can easily create more problems than it solves. Misadventures in measurement often make subsequent endeavors that much more difficult to undertake. "We tried that here and it did not work." A good illustration is in a classic W.C. Fields movie where he entices a "mark" into a game of cards. The soon-to-be-victim says, "A game of chance?" In his famous stage whisper, Fields says "Not the way I play it." Examples abound for things that were "tried here and didn't work." Total quality management (TQM), benchmarking, business process reengineering (BPR), and numerous other approaches would fit this improvement opportunity characterization where the appropriate response is *"not the way we played it."*

NOTE

1. W.E. Deming, *Out of the Crisis* (Cambridge, MA: MIT Center for Advanced Engineering Study, 1986).

CHAPTER 2

What Is Measurement?

Understanding measurement is the key to acceptance and cooperation for an effective outcome. Measurement has a structure, with each of its elements working together to form a system. Why some things are done and why others are not done is not always apparent to everyone. Effective use is encouraged, while misuse is obvious and discouraged. Most often, problems arise with measurement programs not because measurement is not beneficial, but because abuse causes harm to the organization and the people who make up the organization.

WHAT ARE MEASURES?

Measures are analogous to the hierarchy of data:

Information
↓
Knowledge
↓
Wisdom.

Data are the basis of a measurement program. In general, measures have some:

- Quantitative elements (a number—e.g., 42, 127)
- Qualitative elements (e.g., high, heavier, warmer)
- Unit-defined elements (e.g., degrees Fahrenheit, inches, pounds)
- Unit-less elements (e.g., a weighting factor).

To be rigorous, consideration should be directed toward several properties of measures in evolving effective measurement. The key ones are precision, accuracy, and validity:

- **Precision** is the degree to which a measure exactly expresses the property being measured; e.g., inches are a more precise measure of length than are feet.
- **Accuracy** is the property of a measure that describes the extent to which the measure value represents the property value being measured.

The measurement method often determines accuracy. "Stepping-off" a distance is generally less accurate than using a measuring tape; however, the way the measure is taken also affects its accuracy.

- **Validity** is an evaluation of a measure's capability to express the property being measured. For example, in software engineering projects, lines of code are not a valid measure of software size where size is related to the amount of work required to develop, maintain, or support that amount of software product.

Some other properties of measures that should be considered are whether the measure is direct or indirect. For example, a *direct measure* of an object's weight is the reading from the scale on which it is placed. To obtain the weight of that same object, the *indirect measure* would be obtained by measuring its volume and multiplying that result by the density of the object.

In addition, measures are hard or soft. *Hard measures* are based on some physical or determinative property of what is being measured, whereas *soft measures* are based on opinion or perceptions. For example, today's temperature compared to yesterday's would be a hard measure that would tell if today was warmer, cooler, or the same. If several people were asked if they thought today was warmer, cooler, or about the same as yesterday, their answers would be a soft measure of the comparative temperature.

WHAT ARE METRICS?

Continuing with the hierarchy view, metrics are the information dimension of measurement. A *metric* comprises one or more measures. Consider the example of the measure of the width of a 30-inch desk. That is certainly a property of the desk; it has quantification and units. However, this measure takes on a distinct meaning if the desk is being moved to another area and the narrowest part of the move is a 32-inch doorway. Now, the measure has meaning, or as we are defining it, *metric*. Usually metrics combine more than one measure, such as dollars per month or more complex formulas such as earned value analysis (EVA).

Metrics obviously inherit the precision, accuracy, and validity of the measures they comprise, with the metrics' same properties limited to the lowest of these attributes for the associated measures. *Focus* and *coverage* are two additional characteristics of metrics that must be considered in evolving effective measurement.

Measurement can focus on process improvement, progress, benchmarking, project management, technology management, etc. The selected *focus* defines the structure of the measurement activities. For example, if the purpose of measurement is competitive benchmarking, there is little need to define boundaries internal to the overall activity that is being benchmarked. If the focus of measurement is process improvement, then boundaries need to be defined carefully to ensure that processes are compared and analyzed separately and that all data collected take these boundaries into consideration. Clearly, the focus of measurement is a primary determining factor of the cost and speed with which measurement can be implemented.

Coverage expresses how much of what is being measured is actually measured. In situations where all possible measures are taken, the results are called *population measures* or *full coverage.* Measures of less than the full population are *samples;* coverage is then expressed as the sample percentage of the total population. Coverage is also a primary determinant in the overall cost of measurement.

Metrics can also be characterized into four scales:
1. Nominal
2. Ordinal
3. Interval
4. Ratio.

Nominal measures define categories and relationships. Examples of nominal measures are: mode (most frequent occurrence) of a sample, name of a category, and characterization as "temperature." Nominal measures for hair color, for example, would be: brown, blonde, red, black, white/gray, and none of the above (N/A).

Ordinal measures are those given to preserve the ranking of categories. For example, a statement that blonde hair is the second most common natural hair color in the company gives no indication of how many people are in the company or how many blondes there are. It simply states that blonde hair is second.

Interval measures look at relationships between measured objects but preserve the order and magnitude of the relationship. For example, it is 20 degrees warmer today than it was yesterday. An interval measure of the hair colors in the company is that there are 12 fewer blondes than there are people with brown hair but 6 more than there are people with red hair.

Ratio measures preserve the order of the relationship, the magnitude of the interval, and the magnitude of the measure itself. For example, if it is 60 degrees Fahrenheit today and it was 40 degrees Fahrenheit yesterday, the nominal measure is temperature, the ordinal measure is warmer, the interval measure is 20 degrees Fahrenheit warmer, and the ratio measure is 60 degrees Fahrenheit today compared with 40 degrees Fahrenheit yesterday. The thermometer reading is absolute in that there is a zero reference on the Fahrenheit scale and an absolute zero reference related to the Fahrenheit scale.

CHARACTERIZATION OF METRICS BY PURPOSE

Metrics used in organizations can be further characterized by which aspect of the organization is being measured. These aspects generally relate to the efficiency, effectiveness, or health of the organization.

Efficiency measures are by far the most common types of measures found in organizations. A few examples are:

- Are we doing things right?
- What is the return on our investment?
- What is the productivity?

Another bit of measurement wisdom says, "What gets measured gets done." Most evaluation and reward systems are based on efficiency measures.

Too often, efficiency measures overshadow good effectiveness measures. *Effectiveness* is doing the right thing. For example, the right thing might be minimizing inventory or minimizing the number of set-ups in a production line. Set-ups take time and efficiency is measured as units produced per unit time; therefore, it is efficient to produce a minimum number of units each time a set-up is made and it is not effective if most of those units go to inventory. Great care must be taken in measurement program design to avoid what Peter Drucker calls "bifurcation of sub-unit interest groups" or the creation of interests within individual sub-units counter to the organization's interests.[1] Goldratt and Cox illustrate this clearly, using an example where "making the numbers" spawned by well-meant but ultimately counterproductive factory and equipment utilization metrics and goals helped the cost accounting performance, but detracted from the company's overall performance. Fortunately, Goldratt explains how to avoid these types of problems with his Theory of Constraints tools.[2]

The third category, *health*, has only recently been elevated to high importance. The health of an organization or part of an organization describes the ability of the organization to repeat and learn from past performance and improve present and future performance. This concept is also often called *resilience*. Senge discusses the traditional four management disciplines—planning, organizing, staffing, and controlling—and then outlines the need for measuring the organization's ability to learn or become a learning organization.[3]

The converging of three major trends—the globalization of the economy, general economic volatility, and the decrease in the size of the workforce's growth—has made it incumbent on organizations to do more with less in a manner that ensures that they will be able to perform in the future. The success of a project is minimal if the team all leaves when the project is finished. Sustaining success is difficult, especially in current times of "brain drain"—when key talent and skill are easily recruited away. Health metrics monitor this aspect of organizational concern.

When looking at existing measurement programs, it is often tempting to identify a fourth category: *trivial pursuit*. There are surprising numbers of measures and metrics that relate meaningless or incorrect information, but continue for the reason that "it has always been done this way." It should be noted that the name of this category is misleading, since these types of measures are rarely trivial with respect to their cost or their impact.

THE BUILDING BLOCKS OF MEASUREMENT

Looking at measurement as a structure of building blocks is helpful in understanding what effective measurement is and why so many measurement programs fail. The foundation has two blocks to represent what is measured (see Figure 2-1):

1. **Activities**—things that consume resources such as tasks or projects

---

FIGURE 2-1   The Building Blocks of Measurement

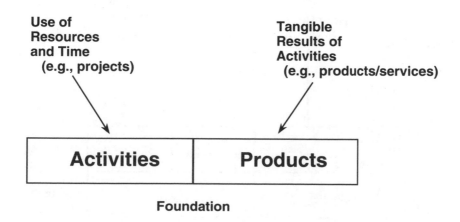

---

2. **Products**—things that are the tangible results of the consumption of resources.

On the first level of this foundation are the measures that quantitatively describe products and activities. Resting on them are four blocks (see Figure 2-2):

1. *Size* measures
2. *Quality* measures
3. *Resource use and timing* measures
4. *Attribute* measures.

Function points are the best example of a *size* measure. The function point index is a measure of a software project or application size based on a quantitative analysis of the functionality provided by its user. Size measures describe how big or how much, and apply to both activities and products. *Quality* measures include defects or other indicators of product goodness. *Resource* use is measured in hours and dollars, and includes the timing of hours and dollars consumed by an activity. *Attribute* measures, like size measures, apply to both products and activities. Attributes are those characteristics of an activity or product that influence the value of a metric.

Three categories of metrics corresponding to the generalized better, faster, and cheaper goals of a metrics program comprise the next level (see Figure 2-3). *Quality* tells us how good our products or services are as a basis for evaluating excellence. The *timing* components of resource use measure

---

FIGURE 2-2   Measures

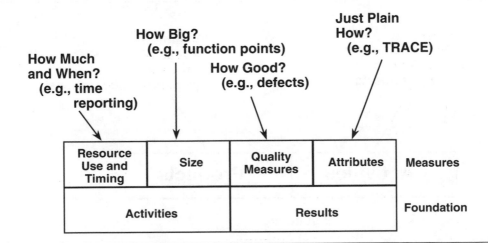

FIGURE 2-3   Metrics

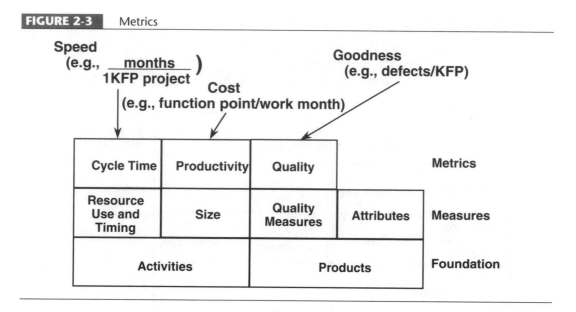

how long it takes to provide products and services as a gauge for speed. *Productivity* metrics note how much per hour or per unit cost, and gauge cheaper, using size information to normalize results.

Note that there is no element that corresponds to the attributes measure, because these metrics tell only what happened, not how it happened or why it happened. Arguably, the most common reason for measurement failure is that most programs stop at this point without trying to understand the results, and therefore, ultimately be able to control the results. Too many metrics programs go no further—giving a good sense of what is happening but no real insight into why it is happening or how to improve performance. It should be noted that attributes do not play a part in the building of the metrics.

The next level is the key to the success of an improvement program. It has only one block: performance standards (see Figure 2-4). Performance standards development is analyzing metric variation against attribute data to determine the effect of each attribute on the metric result. For many reasons, this process is complicated and requires different skills and tools than at any other point in the measurement process. Fortunately, plenty of qualified support is available. Organizations with successful measurement activity hire or obtain the services of qualified measurement professionals to ensure that these complex challenges are carried out correctly.

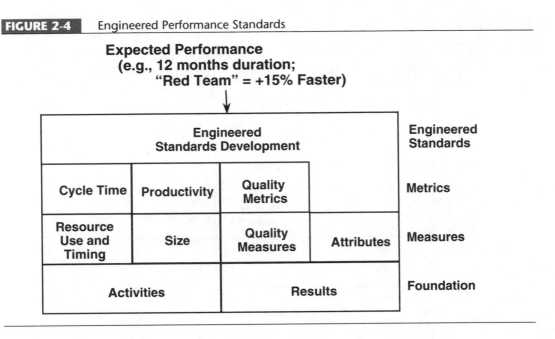

FIGURE 2-4   Engineered Performance Standards

Engineered performance standards make possible the analysis of variation represented by the two blocks in the top row (see Figure 2-5):

1. Common cause variation analysis
2. Special cause variation analysis.

Common cause analysis looks at expected performance for any activity based on its attributes. For example, if a team of known capability and capacity is used, working in an environment of known influences on its performance, and using previously measured tools and techniques to perform the tasks assigned, then historical data should be available and analyzed to provide accurate estimation parameters for this activity without having to consider special causes.

Special cause analysis looks at deviations in an activity's actual performance compared with expected performance (the second definition of productivity). Out-of-tolerance deviations are analogous to out-of-control deviations on a statistical process control chart and indicate the need for investigation. If, after first glance at the data and analysis, an unexpected deviation is still indicated, it must be determined if there is a problem that needs to be fixed or accounted for, or if there are some variations in the performance that are not accounted for in the expectation calculation.

Improvement activities focus on identifying best practices indicated by the engineered performance standards for attributes. Experiments, or

FIGURE 2-5 Special Cause and Common Cause Analysis

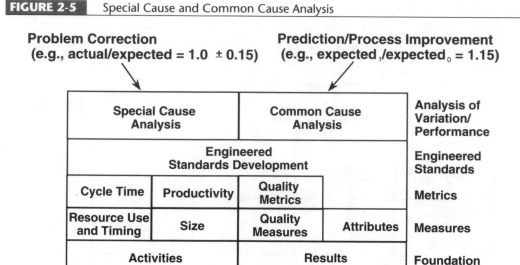

activities that have attributes not included in measured activities, evaluate potential innovations.

Figure 2-6 summarizes the building blocks and their relationships. Remember that the bottom three levels represent the cost of measurement and the creation of data. The top two levels represent turning the data into information and knowledge to realize benefits from measuring and measurement.

CRITICAL SUCCESS FACTORS FOR A MEASUREMENT PROGRAM

Several aspects of a measurement program are critical to its success. These critical success factors (CSF), as defined by Stoner, require that a measurement program be:

- Accurate
- Timely
- Objective and comprehensible
- Focused on strategic control points
- Economically realistic
- Organizationally realistic
- Coordinated with work flow
- Flexible
- Prescriptive and operational
- Acceptable.[4]

FIGURE 2-6 Summary of Building Blocks and Their Relationships

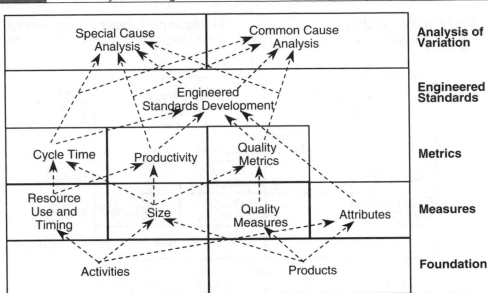

Accurate is used here to collectively describe the properties of accuracy, precision, and validity. To the organization, it can be considered relevance and fairness. Figure 2-7 shows a technical view of accuracy for a software engineering example using size measures as an estimator of work.

Timely means that the results of measurement are available when needed. If measurement is to support decisions, the measurement must be available before the decision needs to be made. The term "post-mortem" applies to how certain activities are reviewed to obtain lessons learned and identify best practices, in addition to several other laudable reasons. Far too often, we can only do post-mortems because the information is not available soon enough to use during the course of the project or activity.

Objective and comprehensible measurement depends on the users of the measures as much as on the measures themselves. The selection of what data to collect and metrics to create is important, but the education of those involved is just as important.

Figure 2-8 shows how the level of understanding of a problem is essential to effective communication. For example, customers understand the business process and need to have some portion of it automated by software engineers who understand the technology of computer systems and applications. The automation or systems development process is a series of translations

FIGURE 2-7 A Technical View of Accuracy

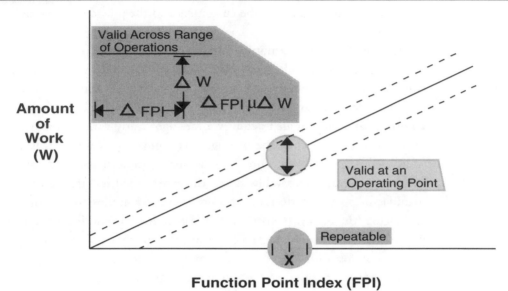

Amount
of
Work
(W)

Valid Across Range
of Operations

$\triangle$ W

$\triangle$ FPI

$\triangle$ FPI $\mu \triangle$ W

Valid at an
Operating Point

Repeatable

X

Function Point Index (FPI)

FIGURE 2-8 Common Understanding of Project

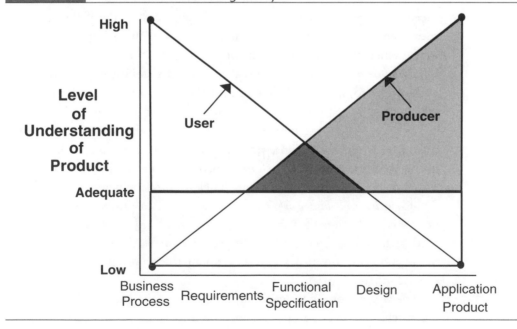

Level
of
Understanding
of
Product

High

Adequate

Low

User

Producer

Business
Process

Requirements

Functional
Specification

Design

Application
Product

from business language to machine language where only at some interim levels of translation can both the customers and the providers communicate effectively.

Chapter 5 contains a normalization method to convert several metrics to key performance indicators (KPI) that greatly improve the ability to communicate the message contained in the metrics without confusing the message with the details of the metrics. Six Sigma is another example of using a normalization technique to convey a message clearly with inconsequential details to the recipient of the message. Six Sigma, at its simplest, is a way of normalizing quality measures so that quality performance and variation can be measured comparably across different activities. If, for example, manufacturing were performing at 4 sigma and accounting were performing at 5 sigma (the higher, the better), the organization would focus on quality improvement efforts and resources toward the manufacturing area as being the greatest area with opportunity for improvement.

Focused on strategic control points requires looking at your vision, mission, and goals, and recognizing that measurement must be integrated with overall direction if measurement is to succeed and if the vision is going to be realized. If part of your vision is to be the best-quality producer in the industry, you need quality measures as well as measures that support decisions to improve quality.

Economic reality says that the benefits of using measurement should exceed the cost. Measurement in itself is pure cost. Only if the results of measurement are used to direct changes that result in improvement can measurement be an astute investment.

Organizational reality requires alignment of visibility, responsibility, and authority. Also, it is inevitable that measurement spawns quantitative goals, which must be realistic. More importantly, it must be recognized that there are only two ways to change the numbers: change the process the numbers reflect, or fraud (intentional or otherwise). A goal or target without the means to change the process (money, people, and time) invites either fraud (innocuously called "gaming") or an attack on measurement.

Coordination with workflow requires change to procedures so that the necessary collection of data is a regular part of any task. Where data are used, analysis and reporting must be precedent steps. Also, if data are used to detect problems, the analysis must be timely to ensure that corrective action can be initiated.

Flexibility is one of the most important but often ignored key elements of measurement success. To understand the importance of flexibility, consider the key concept that doing the same thing over and over will give the same results. Measuring the same process over and over will add substantially to the cost of measurement but will not add to the information gained beyond what is gained by measuring an appropriate sample.

Prescriptive and operational means that measurement gives you insight into changes for improvement and that the indicated changes are feasible. Therefore, the measurement program must indicate not only *what*, e.g., product quality, productivity, or cycle time, but also *why* these values are what they are or why they are different for different processes. If measurement indicates why project A is more productive than project B, maybe project B can be changed in time to improve its results, thereby ensuring that the improved process will be used in future projects. Not only must it be the right prescription, but it must be in a form that can be administered.

Acceptability of measurement is also critical. In measurement it is common to "reinvent the wheel"; in other words, start out fresh and build measurement from the ground up, notwithstanding the availability of many successful models. There is nothing wrong with reinventing the wheel, as long as the result is somewhat round and sized right; some indispensable principles must be accommodated and some fatal flaws must be avoided. Professional help may ensure your success. The method used to get to a potentially successful plan isn't important; educating everyone involved so that it is accepted before it is implemented is essential.

This chapter has systematically progressed from discussions about what measures and measurement programs are to what makes a measurement program successful. The more that is known about each of these factors, the greater chance of having the measurement program return the expected value on investment.

NOTES

1. P. Drucker, *Management: Tasks, Responsibilities, Practices* (New York: Harper & Row, 1974).
2. E. Goldratt and J. Cox, *The Goal: A Process of Ongoing Improvement* (Great Barrington, MA: North River Press, 1985).
3. P. Senge, *The Fifth Discipline: The Art and Practice of the Learning Organization* (New York: Currency/Doubleday, 1994).
4. J.A. Stoner, *Management* (Englewood Cliffs, NJ: Prentice-Hall, 1978).

CHAPTER 3

Levels of Measurement

F ar too often, measurement fails because of a "one size fits all" approach. At least three measurement programs must be in place for measurement to succeed: an executive or strategic level, a management or tactical level, and a task or technical level. It is important to remember that the purpose of measurement is to inform. Informed decisions enable some type of action to be taken; what is not quite as obvious but equally essential is that measurement can beneficially support the decision *not* to act. For measurement to fulfill this role, it must be focused at the level at which the decision is made or where the assurance that no action is needed lies.

One way to characterize the different measurement programs is to consider the decision support in a time perspective. Most executive decisions affect the relatively distant future. Decisions must be made, for example, about a two-, five-, or ten-year plan. Long-range forecasts, next year's budgets, and multiyear projects fill the executive's decision agenda. Contrast this with the line manager's short-term focus on the current quarter's budget or this month's performance, or a worker's attention to the current task.

EXECUTIVE MEASUREMENT PROGRAM

Who has not heard something to the effect of "just give me the bottom line"? Most often, the request comes from upper management or someone with aspirations of upper management. The "big picture" is a concept echoed throughout boardrooms and offices continually.

Considering the perspective of the properties of measurement, what implications would apply to executive metrics in terms of their validity, accuracy, and precision? *Validity* is a binary property of measures: they are either valid or not. A good example is the tenuous relationships of all of the parameters in weather forecasting models. As long as the ocean surface temperature and temperature patterns remain close to their values when all the forecasting models were made, certain parameters such as air pressure gradients are valid predictors of near-term weather. Too often, the term "accurate" is used when what is meant is "valid." When the ocean temperatures changed due to El Niño, many of the parameters that drive the forecast models were no longer valid, and the forecasts were incorrect. Yet validity is still expressed as a confidence interval where there is a certain percentage of confidence that the measure lies within a certain range or has a certain relationship to the inferences that are relying on the measure. Although there are no rules, most executives are uncomfortable if the confidence interval expressed as a percentage is below about 70 percent.

Accuracy is another consideration that contrasts the executive measurement program with the others. One description that is often used when discussing far too much measurement effort is: "Measure it with a micrometer, mark it with a grease pencil, and cut it with an ax." It is funny until one really considers what these micrometers and their use cost. People are usually uncomfortable dealing with imprecise numbers. A schedule to the nearest day may give a greater sense of comfort than one to the nearest month. However, the effort needed to produce the more detailed estimate may be considerably more than the effort needed to produce a general estimate even though a general estimate would satisfy the need for a schedule estimate at the time it is taken.

Translate that into a cost of accuracy and it is obvious why measurement activity fails for cost reasons. The nearest calendar quarter for time measures, or the nearest hundred dollars for cost measures, for example, are typically at the level of accuracy needed to support executive decisions. It is also important to note that any metric is only as accurate as the least accurate measure from which it is developed, no matter how precisely it is stated.

Precision, the level of detail of the metric, also needs to be consistent with accuracy. To say that a project will be complete on Friday at noon two years from today, plus or minus three months, may sound silly; however, far too often, precise measures are given to the nearest month that have an accuracy to the nearest quarter or to the dollar or nearest hundred dollar precision with an accuracy to the nearest ten thousand dollars.

Measurement malpractice, notwithstanding outright fraud, usually lies in problems with the validity, accuracy, and precision of the measures and metrics used to support decisions.

Another key observation about the executive measurement program is that virtually none of the measures or metrics directly originates from or is constructed at the executive level. The measures come from lower levels in the organization; in "rolling up" to the executive level, metrics are aggregated among the several activities and organizational units that contribute to the overall operation of the organization.

MANAGEMENT MEASUREMENT PROGRAM

For our purposes, the management measurement program is the most important. Project managers, department managers, and process or functional managers must all make informed decisions that have an immediate or near-immediate and direct impact on the performance of the part of the organization for which they are responsible. These decisions usually also have at least an indirect impact on other parts of the organization. Compared to executive measures, most managers deal with a time frame that is limited to the present and the immediate or near future.

The accuracy of management measures generally needs to be greater than the accuracy of executive measures. The independence of measures and metrics is higher for managers than for executives. For example, a headcount growth measurement will also impact specific office space and equipment considerations. At lower levels of detail such as at the management level, if a program must be completed in two years, certain things within some departments or projects must be done now or in the very near future.

At the managerial level, for example, payments are made, bills are cut, and taxes are calculated, all of which must be precise to the nearest penny (or appropriate lowest unit of currency). Even where lower levels of precision are acceptable, in general, the managerial level measures need to be at a much higher level of precision than do most executive measures. Many measures are comparisons, such as actual to budget. At executive levels, where many individual budgets are precise to the nearest thousand dollars as they are rolled up to include many budgets for executive decision support, the precision also is reduced to reflect the cumulative effect of the combined uncertainty and the level at which the executives make their decisions.

To illustrate the concept simply, consider if there were 10 department budgets of $10 million each and accurate to 10 percent (or plus or minus $10,000). Therefore, expressing these budgets to anything more precise than the nearest $10,000 dollars is inappropriate. When all these budgets are rolled up, there is $100 million in the total and a combined inaccuracy of plus or minus $100,000. It is still plus or minus 10 percent accuracy, but the precision is now to the nearest $100,000.

TACTICAL MEASUREMENT PROGRAM

The lowest level of the measurement program is at the tactical level. This level will have the highest variability, since it supports the actual performance of tasks and the execution of processes. People and equipment operating at this level usually need a lot of information to ensure that the right tasks are carried out and that they are performed correctly. At this level, the source of the measures, the construction of the metrics, and the communication of the results are all at the same level. These measures can be very effective without much formality.

An important reason to have a good measurement program is the information available concerning any data item before it is reported. If the reported data are inconsistent with the expectation, then the data should be investigated. Most often the first things checked and the most common causes of discrepancies are errors in the data. Once the data have been checked and determined to be correct, if a discrepancy between the expectation and the value still exists, then an investigation is warranted.

One of the primary purposes of a measurement program is to effectively allocate the scarce resources available to fix problems by ensuring that a problem gets fixed at its source. Another key advantage of good measurement is the ability to distinguish the need to fix a problem from a need to fix the process.

Table 3-1 compares the validity, accuracy, and precision requirements for each of the three general measurement programs. It is worthwhile to note that high validity is very important at all levels. Invalid measures support invalid decisions. Slang for the wrong precision is "gnat's eyebrow" or "picky"; slang for low accuracy is "close enough"; while invalidity is usually referred to as "apples and oranges." So make sure your measurements are "in the right church" (valid), "in the right pew" (accurate), and you are "in the right seat," "singing the right hymn," and "on key" (precise). As we will see in Chapter 4, treating measurement as a service by identifying the right customers and incorporating their requirements ensures that all three levels are appropriately covered.

TABLE 3-1   Requirements for Measurement Programs

	Validity	Accuracy	Precision
Executive	High	Moderate	Low
Management	Very High	High	Moderate
Tactical	Very High	Very High	High

Customers of Measurement

There should be a reason or purpose for performing measurement. Measurement is—and should be—first on the chopping block for cost cutting if there are not (1) a legitimate customer for the output of measurement activity, and (2) a legitimate purpose for applying resources to produce those outputs. Successful measurement is similar to any successful product. Sometimes, the product succeeds because it satisfies a need; other times, the product succeeds because it creates its own demand. Nevertheless, at all times, both supply and demand are necessary for success.

The reason most measurement programs fail is not because they failed to do things right, but because they failed to do the right thing. The primary purpose of measurement is to communicate. Obtaining information from its source and delivering it in a form and format that can be used is the primary purpose of a measurement program.

STAKEHOLDER ANALYSIS

Communication always has three elements: the sender, the message, and the receiver. Far too often, measurement programs address only the first two. Senior management requests metrics and an individual or group is given the task of coming up with the metrics program. Procedures and directives ensue. Typically, existing data are discovered and then fashioned into reports distributed via paper reports, a control room, or a web site. Quickly, those assigned to do the measurement become too busy to even identify additional measurement customers and requirements. In addition, those who were initially interested in the measurement outputs lose interest quickly if the reports continually tell the same story. Unless it is recognized that the customers of measurement are the stakeholders and not the senior managers who initiated the measurement request, the measurement effort is likely to result in failure.

Stakeholder analysis ensures that the receiver of the message is identified and participates in the definition of the message. The discussion of the quality function deployment (QFD) approach to ensure the effectiveness of measurement activity has been inspired by a presentation by Gonzalo Verdugo on the audience analysis method.[1] QFD is a process in which the quality features of a product or service are displayed in a matrix with the physical or tangible features of that product or service. The relationships between these two perspectives are then mapped, with the result being the assurance that the physical product or service will deliver the required quality features and functions.

The following is an approach that the author has used with several clients. It is usually customized for each one, providing an opportunity for measurement to address everyone's needs and not only those of big or vocal customers. Another distinct advantage of this approach is that while measurement in most organizations is an integral part of most initiatives, including Total Quality Management (TQM) or Six Sigma, such initiatives are ongoing concurrently, with the resultant measurement being redundant or conflicting. By using this approach, efficient and effective measurement activities can be identified that fully support the concurrent initiatives.

A *stakeholder* is someone who can influence the outcome of what is being measured and/or has an interest in the outcome. For example, the director of finance may exercise considerable influence over the outcome of a project by freezing or releasing funds, although his or her interest in a particular project is probably insignificant, because there is always another project to take its place. In contrast, imagine an end-user line manager with a very high interest in the project but who has little or no influence. When the project is released, it may significantly impact that person's area, for example, in increased training requirements, changes in staffing levels, and learning curve considerations. In addition, project team members may have both high influence and high interest. Figure 4-1 shows the classification of stakeholders. Conceptually, stakeholders in quadrants 2, 3, and 4 must be considered in designing the measurement program.

The *purpose of measurement* is a stakeholder's objective in identifying an information requirement. Essentially, a stakeholder's purpose is the articulation of his or her role with respect to the project. Without using this type of formality, documentation and implementation will not occur. Surprisingly, many reasons similar to, "Because I said so," pervade existing measurement programs. With documentation, political reasons or counterproductive reasons—such as keeping tabs on other workers' activity or singling out individuals for disciplinary action—usually disappear; if they are legitimate reasons, the scrutiny ensures implementation and fair communication.

FIGURE 4-1   Stakeholder Analysis

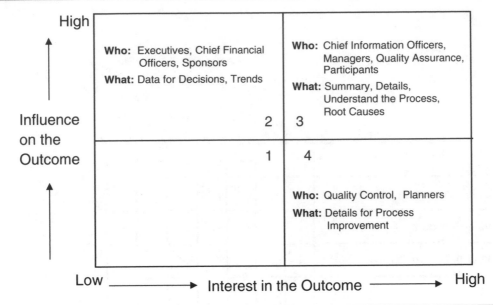

For example, the director of finance focuses on controlling expenditures and keeping informed on costs already incurred as well as for projects currently underway. A project sponsor needs this same information. Other information may not be as obvious but is just as important. For example, a forecast of receivables is necessary so a warehouse manager can plan space effectively, or a human resources manager needs to be informed about specific skills necessary for assignments to ensure focused and timely recruiting. Each of these persons certainly meets the definition of a stakeholder and can clearly articulate his or her purpose for receiving the information.

The mechanics of stakeholder analysis allow the *optimization* of each of the requirements. Clearly, the need of the director of finance for current and planned expenditures is the same as that of the project sponsor, except that the director's need is for all projects and not just one. Clearly, there is enough similarity in meeting the needs for all project sponsors that the need of the director of finance is inherently met. The deployment matrix shown in Figure 4-2 allows this type of efficiency to be realized and offers an opportunity to clarify each stakeholder's purpose in the context of the collective purposes of all stakeholders. With a little experience, this analysis is also helpful in identifying those purposes that are present but that are not assigned or reflected in anyone's perception of his or her role.

FIGURE 4-2 Deployment Matrix

Stakeholder / Purpose	Measure Quality Performance	Monitor Quality Trends	Monitor Development Cost	Measure Productivity	Monitor Productivity Trends	Compare Division Productivity	...
Chief Executive Officer, Executive	✔	✔	✔	✔	✔	✔	
Chief information Officer		✔	✔	✔			
Vice-Presidents, Directors			✔	✔	✔		
Information Technology Quality	✔	✔			✔		
...							

Another important, but often overlooked, aspect of the purpose of measurement is *time consideration.* Some measures need to be made on an ongoing basis, but many others may need to be made only once or premised on a significant nonperiodic event. A substantial opportunity for efficiency exists if the time aspects of these measurement activities can be identified and applied so that measurement is made only "in the right amount, at the right time, and in the right place."

METRICS THAT SATISFY A PURPOSE

Once purposes are identified, the actual metrics or information that the measurement program provides enables the stakeholder to draw conclusions for the project based on the metrics. A report showing the total dollars spent or committed each month for all projects would appear to satisfy the director of finance's purpose. Of course, other information also applies. How accurate does the information need to be? Does it need to be to the nearest penny, or the nearest hundred thousand dollars? Does it need to be broken out by project, department, or geographic region? It is essential to answer all these questions. Using the communications metaphor, the receiver is defining the requirements for content and format of the message for the sender.

The mechanics are the same as in the association of stakeholders with their purposes. The deployment matrix shown in Figure 4-2 allows this type of efficiency to be realized and again offers an opportunity to clarify with each stakeholder his or her messages in the context of the collective reporting to all stakeholders. This also offers tremendous opportunity for efficiency if a stakeholder can identify common reporting that will satisfy the purpose.

MEASURES THAT COMPRISE A METRIC

In keeping with our definition of metrics as comprised of one or more measures, a deployment matrix of the measures associated with the metrics is identified in Figure 4-3. It is also apparent from this activity that it is extremely efficient if redundant data collection is eliminated.

FIGURE 4-3 Deployment Matrix—Metrics

Purpose \ Metric	Dollars per Function Point	Defects per Function Point	Person Months per Function Point	Total Development Dollars			
Measure Quality Performance		✔					
Monitor Quality Trends		✔					
Monitor Development Cost	✔			✔			
Measure Productivity			✔				
Monitor Productivity Trends			✔				

Here is where the specific requirements for measures are identified, such as timing, coverage, units of measure, accuracy, and precision. Also, the assignments of responsibility for the collection, as well as the means for communicating the data, can be identified here.

THE MEASUREMENT PLAN

The last step in the stakeholder analysis is the creation of the *measurement plan* that provides the details of what measures will be taken, where they will be taken, how they will be taken, and when they will be taken. Remember, the preceding step of identifying the purposes for each stakeholder answers the "why" for each resultant activity. It is important to note that this process eliminates the most significant traditional reason—"because we always have"—for measurement in most organizations, and consequently the biggest measurement dollar and opportunity cost.

To develop the measurement plan, the measures identified in the previous steps are evaluated as "available" or "not available" (see Figure 4-4). From this information, data collection, communication, and analysis requirements can be identified and assigned. The greatest advantage to most organizations is that data identified in the deployment matrices previously created can be

---

FIGURE 4-4   Developing the Measurement Plan

Measure	Available?	
	Yes	No
Application Function Points		✔
Defects after Deployment (90 days)		✔
Project Labor	✔	
Project Function Points		✔
Project Cost	✔	
Release Open Defects	✔	
Inspection Defects		✔

eliminated if they are not used. Far too often, the observation that measurement is expensive can be traced to the collection of data that are not used, but cannot be identified as such by those responsible for its collection and, consequently, its cost.

The success of measurement, like the success of so many things, does not depend on what you do, but on how well you satisfy the needs of your customers. The customers of measurement are those with an influence or interest in the outcome of an activity who are identified in the first part of the stakeholder analysis. The identification of each stakeholder's purpose, role, or information requirement constitutes the second part of the analysis. Designing the metrics and reports that satisfy the stakeholder's purposes is the third part of the analysis. Remember, the stakeholder decides what it is that satisfies his or her purpose. In the fourth part of the analysis, as the metrics are identified, the data used to create the metrics are also identified. The final step is to create and implement the measurement plan, where available data are identified, requirements for additional data are noted, and activities for collecting data not used are identified and terminated.

The stakeholder analysis process is summarized in Figure 4-5. The design of the measurement program is reflected in the arrows going from the stakeholder analysis at the top down through measure availability. As the measures become available, the communication of data and its conversion to the information needed by the stakeholders will flow back up these arrows.

FIGURE 4-5   The Stakeholder Analysis Process

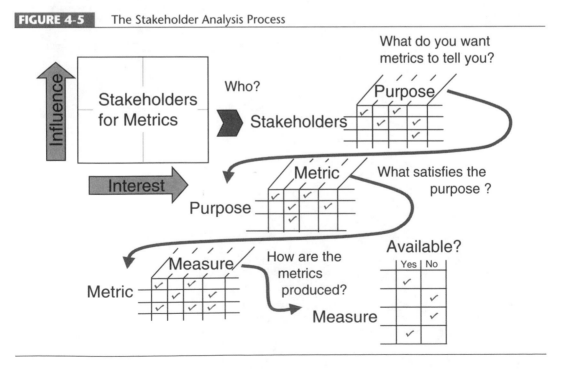

It is very important to note that stakeholder analysis is not a one-time event; it is an ongoing process. If a stakeholder's purpose is satisfied and the information is no longer necessary, then the analysis should be worked through to see if the effort spent collecting the associated measure(s) and producing the reports can be terminated. If a new requirement is identified, it should be worked through to see if existing metrics or measures can satisfy that purpose or if new measures are needed.

NOTE

1. Gonzalo G. Verdugo, *Measurement Program Design: Addressing the Needs of Project and Applicatrion Support Teams*, Rubin and Associates, Presentation to Quality Assurance Institute Ninth International Conferrence, March 20–21, 1991.

CHAPTER 5

Implementing a Measurement Program

I n software engineering, there is an adage that says: "Don't expect miracles, rely on them." There is something similar in measurement: "Don't anticipate resistance, count on it." Measurement enables change—from small changes in tasks to significant changes in culture. The confidence that results from having quantitative information facilitates bold decisions that will have broad effects. Current times have made us more receptive to the idea that change is the rule rather than the exception. Where measurement is perceived as the way to engineer change to our best advantage, acceptance of measurement is much more likely than if change is perceived to be forced upon us.

CHALLENGES

When buying a car, not much time is spent contemplating the alternative theories behind the various models' design differences. Similarly, when buying electronics, not much time is spent exploring the theoretical differences in different products' circuit design. Why is it then that so many workers and their managers get hung up on the technical aspects of any proposed measurement?

There is a serious problem if a thorough understanding of something is required before it can be used. One could not make toast unless electrical resistance and thermal expansion were understood, or watch television unless one understood how the receiver, signal transmission, and program production worked. Considering this, it is difficult to understand why workers and their managers reject or resist measurement efforts, citing a lack of understanding of technical aspects of measurement or mentioning several alternative theories or technologies that can be used for measurement as a premise for doing nothing.

As long as a process' performance is unknown, there is a possibility that it is not performing as well as it could be. Most enlightened management theories state that an unmeasured process is virtually guaranteed to be significantly improvable. Therefore, the introduction of measurement and the subsequent discovery of a significant improvement opportunity will likely reflect negatively on the manager's ability and performance.

Any excuse will do as long as the result is that nothing is measured. If the "do nothing" preferred alternative cannot be avoided, then a measurement method must be selected that can be manipulated to maintain the appearances of competitiveness and improvement independent of actual performance. For most organizations, this changes the measurement problem significantly. The purpose of measurement must be clearly defined so as to avoid finger pointing. The managers or employees who are afraid of damaging their careers or reputations are not those who have failed or performed poorly in the past; rather, it is those who fail to evaluate their performances thoroughly and objectively and fail to strive to improve.

Measurement is a tool that the enterprise must use to:

1. Evaluate its performance thoroughly and objectively
2. Identify improvement opportunity.

The enterprise leaders must provide the measurement tools and insist on their use.

There is a hierarchy of issues (like hurdles) that must be cleared before measurement can succeed (see Figure 5-1). Failure to clear the hurdles is preemptive: The contestant does not win—measurement does not go forward and does not succeed. It is not surprising that those who would benefit most

FIGURE 5-1	Hierarchy of Issues

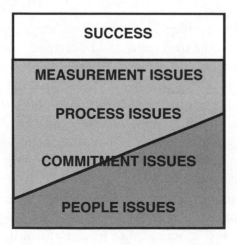

SUCCESS

MEASUREMENT ISSUES

PROCESS ISSUES

COMMITMENT ISSUES

PEOPLE ISSUES

Increasing
Chance of
Success

from an effective measurement system are its biggest opponents. Managing people and change presents greater challenges than measurement.

The first type of issue relates to *people*. People rarely want to be measured. There is an inherent fear, usually based on experience, that measurement will be used against individuals. "Treat me like a person, not like a bunch of numbers." Questions arise like "who will get or not get to see the data?" and "what happens to old data?" The key to successful measurement is giving honest answers to these types of questions. Those answers will determine if the measurement program will proceed.

The second type of issue relates to *commitment* to measure. Commitment issues could be overcome easily if they were only resource-related, but the commitment to measurement as "the way we do things" is essential to success. Evidence abounds that successful measurement is "cheap at any price," that bad measurement is "unaffordable at any cost," and that any well-defined request for commitment to measurement or a response to a directive for a measurement initiative outlining the commitment requirements would be well received. On the other hand, taken by itself, measurement is pure cost. It only takes away from the bottom line. When cost cutting is a priority, measurement is usually one of the first things at risk. To ensure that commitment to measurement continues, the results of measurement must be tied to the bottom line.

Next are *process* issues. If it can't be decided how measurement will be done, it will not get done. It is not a coincidence that many organizations trying to do measurement fail in executing measurement because of problems in executing projects. The planning process is the key to success. Subject matter knowledge is essential in creating a plan that will work. If the project lacks access to people who truly understand the elements of a successful measurement program, don't expect the plans to achieve it to be of much use or value. On the other hand, if the plans are supportive of measurement success, it can be expected that changes necessary to address the process issues will be well supported and easily overcome.

Measurement issues are last set of issues that must be overcome. These issues include: what data will be collected, where they will be collected, how they will be analyzed, how they will be reported, and who can see the data. For most organizations, these are the toughest issues because they relate to the discipline of measurement itself. Measuring a process is different from doing the process. You need professional help for measurement just as you need human resources for staffing or the legal department for licensing products. The difference just isn't quite as obvious.

PLANNING

Implementing measurement is a project—and the key to the success of any project is planning. Having the measurement in place is not the real objective of the measurement project; it is having the measurement used by the organization. After measurement is implemented, if decisions are still made without significant use of the data, then interest and support for the measurement will quickly drop off. Part of measurement planning must include incorporating the measurement data into existing policies and procedures. A significant part of the organization's commitment to measurement is a commitment not to continue to do things in the absence of measurement information.

DATA COLLECTION

There are many options for the collection of data. If the stakeholder analysis is done well, the data to be collected are well specified. Usually the process owners, or those closest to the activity to be measured, will have the best ideas how to collect the needed data. Process design tasks may be necessary to implement the data collection. Usually, an automated process to collect data is preferable to a manual process. To help with ongoing functions of planning, analysis, and justification for the measurement program, it is often helpful to include the cost of data collection in the data reporting.

DATA ANALYSIS

It is rare that data are analyzed using manual processes. In the measurement design process, the measures that produce the metrics and their associated reports are translated into requirements for automated data analysis and the production and delivery of reports. Analyzing the data is not the biggest challenge; it is educating the users of the data what the information means and what it does not mean. Usually, it is not sufficient simply to communicate the data; the meta data (data about the data) must also be communicated. The accuracy, precision (if not obvious), validity, and any other information that might usually be conveyed as footnotes will help the decisionmaker use the data appropriately.

DATA REPORTING

Having the users define the measurement program enables them also to define what the information they receive needs to look like. One of the greatest challenges of measurement is effective communication. Of course, communication is also a guide to the project management body of knowledge (also known as the *PMBOK Guide®*).[1] Beyond merely reporting specific metrics is the problem of communicating metrics to those who do not understand what their value or behavior indicates. Moreover, communicating metrics to those with a solid understanding may also be difficult because they may not understand those metrics in context.

The performance index matrix (PIM) provides a concise format for measuring multiple quantitative and qualitative metrics that represent achievement of an organization's objectives and/or goals over time (see Table 5-1). Among the advantages of the PIM format are that it:

- Measures both quantitative and qualitative aspects of performance on one scale
- Emphasizes results rather than activities
- Identifies most important results through assignment of relative weights
- Integrates performance measures across groups performing disparate functions to provide one overall performance indicator
- Provides understandable ongoing feedback to motivate performance improvement.

The following is the procedure for constructing a PIM:

1. Determine the groups and/or activities to be covered by the matrix and identify the time period that the matrix will cover.
2. Identify the metrics to be included in the PIM.
3. Identify the data requirements for each metric and implement data collection.
4. Evaluate the metrics for the base period.
5. Establish a performance scale for each metric. With the value for the base period at 3, determine reasonable objective and goal values for the metric throughout the time period of the matrix. Then, assign these values to the ascending rating scale. Also, determine values for possible degradation in performance during the time period of the matrix and assign these values to the descending rating scale.
6. Determine weights for each metric. These weights indicate the importance of each metric and are usually assigned by management.
7. For each reporting period, determine the performance index for each metric and the overall index by multiplying each performance index by its respective weight and summing the results.
8. Monitor performance trends through changes in the performance indices and the overall index over time.

TABLE 5-1 Example of a PIM

METRIC	1	2	3	4	5	6		
PERFORMANCE	97.2	2.0	84.5	100.0	15.2	2.4		
	99.4	1.5	100.0	*100.0*	5.0	2.8	10	
	98.8	1.6	98.3	98.8	7.0	2.7	9	
	98.2	1.7	96.6	97.6	10.4	2.7	8	
	97.6	1.8	94.9	96.4	13.1	2.6	7	
	97.0	1.9	93.2	95.2	*15.8*	2.5	6	RATING
	96.5	2.1	91.6	94.1	18.5	2.5	5	SCALE
	96.0	2.2	90.0	93.0	21.2	*2.4*	4	
	95.5	2.4	87.0	91.0	23.4	2.2	3	
	95.0	2.6	84.0	89.0	25.6	2.8	2	
	94.5	2.8	81.0	87.0	27.8	1.9	1	
	94.0	3.0	78.0	85.0	30.0	1.8	0	
	6	5	2	10	6		RATING	
	25	20	20	15	10		WEIGHT	
	150	100	40	150	60		VALUE	

540 INDEX

METRIC:

1 = AVERAGE ON -LINE AVAILABILITY IN % (ALL APPLICATIONS)
2= AVERAGE TOTAL RESPONSE TIME IN SECONDS
   (WEIGHTED BY TRANSACTION TOTALS)
3= PERCENTAGE OF TARGET DATES MET FOR PROBLEMS
4= PERCENTAGE OF CHANGES SUCCESSFUL
5= HELP DESK (% OF CALLS ABANDONED)
6= OVERALL ISD USER PERFORMANCE RATING

9. Review performance trends and, if necessary, adjust the performance scales to reflect changes in processing procedures.

The obvious advantage to using such a method is that it changes the focus from the variations themselves to what is important. The analogy often used is a bag of oatmeal. You can push it in at several places to make it look different, but it always bulges out elsewhere, leaving you with the same amount of oatmeal. Real improvement involves getting more oatmeal into or out of the bag—depending on how the analogy is cast.

PIM Definitions

Index: The sum of all sub-indices which provides a total measure of performance. Since all base period ratings equal 3 and all weights sum to 100, each PIM begins with an overall index of 300.

Metrics: Output or performance indicators identified in consultation with management as reflecting the achievement of desired results.

Rating: The score for the metric in question determined by comparing actual performance to the rating scale created when the metrics goals were entered up and down the index column. Base period ratings should be entered at the level three (3) row of the table for all criteria. So, for the initial period, the total index score should be 300 and subsequent periods will range between 0 and 1,000, depending on the improvement or deterioration in the performance of the metrics being monitored.

Rating Scale: A scale of 0-10 against which values for each metric have been assigned. Ratings of 0 and 10, respectively, define the lower and upper limits of performance.

Sub-Index: The value determined by multiplying a metric's rating by its weight.

Weight: The value indicating the importance identified by management for the metric in question. The sum of all weights equals 100.

This type of tool ensures that only real improvement is reflected in the index. For example, if costs and time are reduced by eliminating quality steps, even though both measures show improvement, there should be an offsetting degrade in the customer rejection rate or customer satisfaction. In the well designed PIM, the index should at least not improve, and probably should show an overall decline if the importance weightings are slanted toward the customer (the "customer focus" so widely professed).

Resistance is a key factor that organizations must address if they are to perform meaningful measurement. In most organizations, measurement falls into the category of cultural change. In many cases, measurement may even raise legal issues where contracts have clauses that address measurement issues and restrict what an organization can or cannot do. It is essential to say up front what the measurement program will and will not do. If those objectives and prohibitions are acceptable to workers and management, and there is sufficient commitment to realize those goals and enforce the rules, success will follow.

NOTE

1. *A Guide to the Project Management Body of Knowledge, 2000 Edition* (Upper Darby, PA: Project Management Institute, 2000).

CHAPTER 6

Measurement Program Maturity

S ome things take money; some things take time; measurement programs take both. When dealing with any product's lifecycle, it is desirable to move quickly to an equilibrium point of getting the desired output with minimum input and then remaining responsive to changes in demand while maintaining high levels of efficiency. This maturing process applies equally to measurement.

EVOLVING A MEASUREMENT PROGRAM

As discussed with regard to moving from unconscious incompetence to conscious incompetence, measurement and its use are an evolutionary process. One of the keys to measurement success is managing evolution effectively so as not to exceed the expectations of an immature program's capability and not to overlook the program's potential at any time as it evolves.

MATURING THE MEASUREMENT PROGRAM

Maturity is a hot topic. As discussed in Chapter 1, Aligning the Facets, measurement can easily be identified as a facet in a maturity model developed for an organization. The key to a maturity model is having certain levels of maturity manifested by critical success factors for each level. There are also certain actions that must be taken to advance each critical success factor ultimately to the next level. An example of a maturity matrix for software engineering measurement follows. Five levels are chosen to correspond to the Software Engineering Institute Capability Maturity Model (SEI CMM®) five-level maturity scale. In actual practice, the number of levels is empirically derived to ensure a significant difference between the levels, and there is a measurable and verifiable improvement associated with advancement to each level. The tasks are shown in Table 6-1.

TABLE 6-1 Measurement Facet for Software Engineering

Maturity Level	Maturity Indicators	Tasks to Move to Next Level
Ad hoc	1. No formal measurements in place	1. Define measurement functions and responsibilities
		2. Establish and implement measurement procedures
		3. Develop and deliver measurement training
		4. Implement function point size measures in existing projects
		5. Size existing portfolios in function points
		6. Implement time and cost collection improvements/procedures
		7. Implement defect data collection
		8. Identify and report key process indicator (KPI) metrics
		9. Establish metric analysis and reporting
Measured	1. Key process areas identified	1. Develop control charts for each KPI metric and for all other metrics as appropriate
	2. Key measurements in place and data collection in process	
	3. Key process indicator reporting established	
	4. Basic estimating processes used	
Improvement	1. Control limits established for key measurements	1. Implement attribute data collection
	2. Estimating and operating decisions supported by measurements and data	2. Develop attribute data analysis
		3. Develop engineered performance standards
	3. Accurate estimating capability established (process-specific delivery rates)	4. Implement process standardization
Standardization	1. Performance prediction of all processes accurate to within 10%	1. Implement design of experiments for innovation
	2. Measurement support required for all project and improvement decisions	
	3. Measurement data used with customers in planning	
Innovation	1. Experiments for improvements routinely conducted within standard processes	

As the measurement program matures, progress can be tracked as shown in Figure 6-1.

Tasks shown as necessary to move to a higher level are indicated at the level at which they need to be completed. To advance in maturity at a reasonable rate, these tasks may need to be started much sooner than when their precedent level is reached. The precedent event necessary for any of the tasks to move to the next level is obtaining a commitment to implement a mature measurement program. So, if the plan were laid out using program evaluation review technique (PERT) methodology, the late start for many of the higher maturity tasks could possibly occur before the finish of any tasks necessary to define a lower level of maturity. Failure to recognize this concept greatly increases the time to reach maturity and greatly increases the risk that the measurement program will fail.

It is frequently argued that there is no point in doing measurement at lower levels of process maturity since everything eventually changes. The truth is that there is considerable, and apparently random, variability in these measures. In general, the more data that are available, the easier it is to analyze variation. Available attribute data facilitate the analysis of variation; having these past data available greatly speeds up the improvement process by increasing the sensitivity of the analysis.

There are two controlling dependencies in maturing the measurement programs: investment and time. *Investment dependency* is, as the name implies, the rate at which the measurement program can mature as limited by the rate of investment in the program. *Time dependency* is the nondiscretionary limitation imposed by the nature of the data. For example, if there is a requirement for a 75 percent confidence interval for data used to improve processes, and it takes 15 data points taken at one-month intervals to achieve

FIGURE 6-1   Tracking Progress of Tasks for Measurement Facet

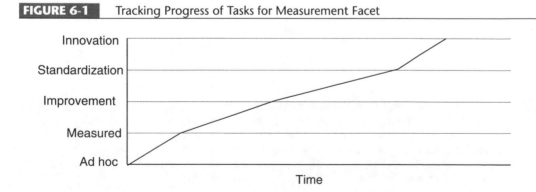

that confidence interval, then it will take at least 15 months to achieve that level. Recognizing these dependencies is important in planning the measurement program and in establishing the expectations for its results.

MAINTAINING THE MEASUREMENT PROGRAM

Maintaining a measurement program is a delicate balancing act of ensuring that the program is perceived as valuable but not wasteful. The key to ensuring that those perceptions are maintained is to continually use the stakeholder analysis tool to capture the evolving requirements of the stakeholders and to identify those requirements that have expired so that support for the expired requirements is discontinued. As mentioned earlier, it is also worthwhile to track the costs associated with the collection and analysis of data. Therefore, the measurement program is also a stakeholder with the legitimate purpose of evaluating the program's effectiveness and benefits. It is an excellent idea to regularly solicit from the other stakeholders information regarding improvements, expanded capabilities, cost savings, and cost avoidance.

FOCUSING THE MEASUREMENT PROGRAM—SPECIAL PROJECTS

Measurement is a powerful tool; therefore, it is desirable to have the capacity to process special requests for analyzing existing data and for collecting and analyzing ad-hoc data. It is reasonable to expect that as the measurement program matures, routine measurements will decrease to a level of mostly monitoring and exception reporting. Responsiveness to such special requests is often key to maintaining the resources necessary to champion the measurement program as it and the organization evolve, and thereby answering the challenges to measurement.

Measurement follows a progression from an initial state, which is usually not very effective and is fraught with problems, to a more mature state of greater effectiveness and fewer consequences with problems. Maturing is not solely a function of the passage of time. People, for example, tend to mature naturally due to basic survival instincts. A measurement program, with no natural influences, however, will move toward maturity only if its operators cause it to do so. It is essential to have a solid definition of what maturity is and a plan to get there.

CHAPTER 7

Quality, Cycle-Time, and Productivity Measures

The vast majority of measurement activity and organizational visions, missions, and goals can be distilled to "the big three": better, faster, and cheaper. This chapter focuses on their manifestation in measurement: quality, cycle-time, and productivity measures. Understanding how to measure these results effectively, how to use them to understand the results, and how to change them will make the difference between success and failure.

Which one should you measure? It sounds like a silly question, but there really is a relationship among the three that offers an efficiency opportunity in establishing and running an overall measurement effort. Most software engineers are familiar with the phrase: "good, fast, cheap; pick two." Each industry has a similar saying. For any given process, there is a relationship among all the parameters (dependent variables) such that managing any two of these will determine the result of the third. This should raise the question of what these variables are dependent on. Each is thought of as an independent variable and one sets out to accomplish things such as improve productivity or quality or reduce cycle-time. In reality, these are results and not controls. The controls are the processes used. After each of the dependent variables of process is reviewed, process and process improvement are discussed.

BETTER: THE MEASUREMENT OF QUALITY

Despite several years of quality revolution, most organizations are still arguing over the definition of quality. Managing quality effectively is still seldom achieved. Usually, quality management is packaged into a program complete with its own definitions, tools, and numerous consultants to help the organization invest heartily to achieve the benefits these programs claim. Examples are total quality management (TQM), advocated by Dr. W. Edwards Deming, and Six Sigma, another popular package usually associated with Motorola and its winning the Baldrige quality award. Taguchi loss function, continuous quality improvement (CQI), and zero defects embody the same principles of doing things right the first time and thereby reducing rework and waste.

For the purpose of improving processes to yield better quality, there must be an assumption that the problem is rooted in the process. If the process is changed, the quality of its output will change. The right change will yield improved quality. Then, to evaluate quality, it is necessary to clearly define operating terms. The words a person actually uses—and those that he or she will find used—may vary, but the concepts they represent must be distinguishable if quality improvement is to be achieved.

Quality improvement is finding and fixing faults. Considerable effort is spent finding and fixing defects (over and over and over). This is only quality control at best, and fighting fires is its most common manifestation. The flow charts in Figures 7-1 through 7-4 show the measurement process to support quality improvement.

However, flow-charting without documenting the properties makes a nice picture but poor tool for process understanding and improvement. Table 7-1 illustrates the symbols used in the following flow charts and the properties associated with each symbol.

Figure 7-1 shows the initiation of a process where the output is to an internal customer and is tested and/or inspected (T & I process) or delivered to an internal customer without testing. The process output includes errors (untested elements), internal defects (note that all errors detected in this

TABLE 7-1 Repetitive Process Flow Charting

Process Flow Charting Symbol		Symbol Properties
Arrow	$\longrightarrow$	Flow volume Flow timing
Input/Output	▱	Naming/responsibility notation
Storage/Queue	▽	Volume Capacity Timing
Operation	▢	Resource use Timing Capacity
Decision	◇	Criteria Flow percentage
Control Point	✔	Point at which a measurement is taken

Definitions

Amount of each type of work done—A measure of the total hours spent for each type of work done.

Attributes—The factors to which common cause variation in measures and metrics is attributed.

Channel—The smallest unit by which work is done. Typically this is a person, but possibly a task team. A channel is the basic unit for capacity of a system.

Defect—The condition in a product or output of a process that must be fixed. Generally, defect is the term used to refer to the condition if it has passed a process step designed to detect it or if it has been released to an external customer (end user).

Delay—A nondiscretionary condition that prevents work from being done.

Error—Another term used to refer to a defect before it has been subject to a process step designed to detect it.

Failure—The manifestation of a defect. Note that one defect can result in many failures or that many defects can be associated with one failure. A failure can occur without the benefit of a defect according to this definition and, conversely, a defect can exist without an associated failure.

Fault—The condition in a process that must be changed to effect the desired change in the process output.

Internal defect—Another term used to refer to a defect after it has passed a process step designed to detect it but before the product containing the defect is released to the customer. Obviously, if the internal defect is undetected, it can only be discussed conceptually. If it is common to detect defects but not fix them before release to the customer, then an additional term for a detected internal defect is required.

Pace—The relative speed of doing work. 1.0 is the normal or standard pace of doing work. Working slower or faster than normal is represented as a percentage of standard pace.

Process— 1. The set of procedures and steps that produce products.

2. The set of attributes used in producing products.

Definition 1 is used in measuring and managing similar products, such as in repetitive manufacturing. Definition 2 is used for customized products, such as in custom manufacturing or in software engineering.

Project—The application of resources and process to produce a product or meet an objective.

Quality— 1. The defect content of a product. It is expressed as defects per function point for software engineering (or other appropriate unit in other fields).

2. Conformance to standards.

3. Fitness for use.

4. A property of a product in which presence and absence are both easy to spot.

Sequence—The order in which things are done. Sequence can be mandatory or discretionary.

Suspense—A discretionary decision not to work on a particular item.

Throughput—The absolute speed of doing work. It represents the total amount of work done in a standard time interval. Throughput considers both pace and capacity.

Total amount of work done—A measure of how much total work was done for the product produced. It is measured in hours for the activity.

Type of work done—The actual scope of the process (e.g., specification, design, code, and test are all types of work done in software engineering). The type of work done should correspond to the intersection of a work breakdown structure describing the tasks to be done and an organization breakdown structure showing the skills necessary to perform the work.

process go through the repair process), and products. There are data for the volume of output tested, the number of errors found, the volume of output not tested, and identification of what was not tested.

Figure 7-2 illustrates the production process. The customer is still an internal customer, but now the possibility has been introduced that a test or inspection will detect an internal defect that was missed in the initiation process. Data have now been gathered at the indicated control points so that in addition to the same data that were available from the initiation process, there are now also data for the number of defects found.

The delivery process where the product is handed over to the end user is illustrated in Figure 7-3. It looks the same as the production process except that additional data are collected concerning what was handed to the customer in its entirety. Remember that once delivery takes place, everything wrong is a defect, even if the process did not include a test and inspection step designed to detect it.

Figure 7-4 shows the product in use. The use can result in a failure; the failures are tested and inspected or evaluated to determine the cause of the failure and then fixed or discarded. The repair process can also introduce errors and deliver defects to the customer in the same manner as did the original production process. The control points provide additional data.

The important conclusion from this series is the information necessary to specifically identify the number of errors the process produced and the efficiency of the process in detecting and removing errors. Too often, organizations measure only part of this quality information. If customer complaints are down, does that mean that quality is improving? Other possibilities are that customers have quit complaining because it did not do any good or that customers are leaving and are no longer there to complain.

The only real gauge of quality improvement is that fewer defects are being introduced because faults have been discovered and repaired. Also, it means that new faults are not being created in the process to introduce new defects. Usually, this type of data is supported with information regarding the severity of failures and ensures that proper focus is placed on the priority of finding and correcting certain faults.

Finally, this type of information ensures that it is possible to distinguish defects and failures caused by special causes of variation (where a special fix to the product is appropriate with no change to the process) from common causes of variation (where a fix to the process is the appropriate action).

FIGURE 7-1 Initiation of a Process

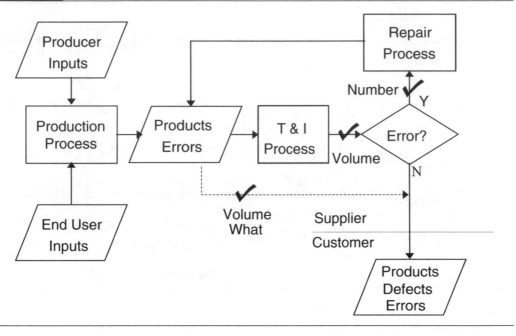

FIGURE 7-2 Production Process

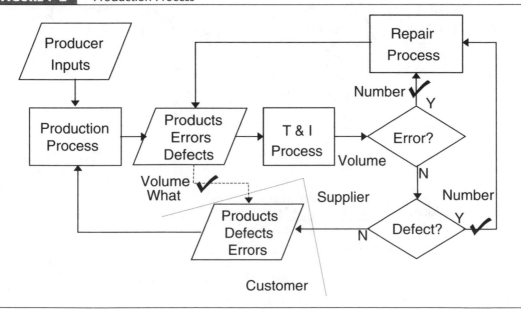

FIGURE 7-3   Delivery Process

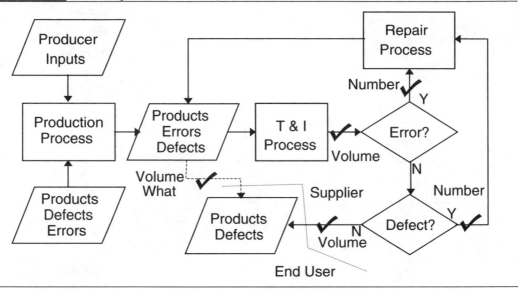

FIGURE 7-4   The Product in Use

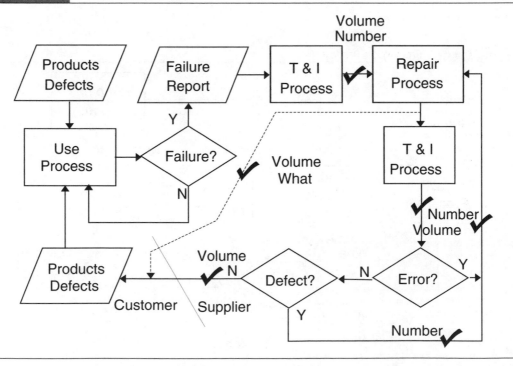

FASTER: THE MEASUREMENT OF CYCLE-TIME

Cycle-time is a popular topic but it is not well understood. It is not uncommon to hear comments like "cycle-time, schedule, whatever you call it." Actually, cycle-time and schedule are completely different concepts. Most measurement activity ignores cycle-time or relegates it to low importance after quality and productivity measurement and management. Of course, improving cycle-time—being faster—is nearly everybody's goal, although it seldom gets more than lip service. Achievement of cycle-time goals becomes a type of "schedule met" metric that reflects how well scheduling (or over-scheduling) is performed. Leaping into cycle-time measurement and reduction without a clear understanding of what that means, which concepts to apply, and where to apply them invites disaster. The following is an explanation of what cycle-time is and what it is not, and how to measure and improve cycle-time in a software engineering environment.

There are two areas of concern in applying cycle-time measures: flow efforts and queuing systems. Projects are flow systems; once the activity has started, it continues until it is completed. Support work is typically a queuing system; customer requests wait for service while work is done using some queuing discipline.

Cycle-Time versus Schedule

It is hard to imagine two things that are so different being confused so often. Cycle-time is a *dependent variable* that is a function of the independent variable process with assumptions about several other independent variables: pace, sequence, throughput, quality, scope of work, delay, suspense, and amount of work done. Schedule is an *independent variable* where other factors are varied dependent on the schedule. Cycle-time is primarily a property of a *process* whereas schedule is a property of a *project* or *activity*. The following analogy should clarify these concepts.

An automobile has a certain design speed. This design speed is based on properties such as the engine and drive system used, certain assumptions about the weight, fuel used, road conditions, weather conditions, and many other factors. By fixing the values for these factors, a fair comparison about the speed capability of automobiles can be made among various models.

The design speed of the automobile is analogous to cycle-time. When the car is driven, the speed at which it goes depends on several factors, including variations in all those factors that were held at a constant value in determining the design speed. Other factors that were not considered in the design speed determination (such as having to stop for fuel or traffic conditions) also influence the speed of the car. The time allotted for the trip is analogous to the schedule. So, in this analogy, design speed (cycle-time) is a property of the car (process), while planned speed (schedule) is limited by the design speed but considers both the design speed and external factors.

Cycle-Time versus Duration

Duration, like schedule, is also a property of a project or activity. Where schedule was the planned time for the project or activity, duration is the actual time that it took. Most measurement programs purporting to measure cycle-time really measure duration. If measurement is to reach its overall guiding principle of understanding the process, cycle-time is a key factor that must be correctly understood and applied.

Much confusion arises from consideration that *cycle-time* has different meanings depending on the context. For product marketing companies, cycle-time may mean *concept to market*. Internally, at the highest levels, cycle-time may mean an *idea (or request) to implement*. To the worker, cycle-time may mean *start to finish* for a task; for the supervisor, it means *assignment to completion*, and may include items sitting on the worker's desk before work is started and after work is completed and then passed on. All these perspectives are correct.

The units of cycle-time measurement are time units, such as hours, days, and weeks. The object of cycle-time measurement is a process—the standard amount of work to be done, and the manner in which the work is to be done. The subject of cycle-time measurement is whatever has meaning to whomever the measure is performed by or for. So, as a customer, cycle-time relates to how long he or she expects to wait, and as a producer, it is relative to how long he or she expects to take.

Real cycle-time measures bear little resemblance to duration or schedule measures. Double shifts, weekend work, SWAT teams, etc., should make things move faster. However, if these are all done using the same process, the cycle-time is the same and only the capacity and throughput are changed. If such tactics result in a different process being used, then a different cycle-time—the one for the process used—applies.

Real cycle-time improvement is real process improvement. While sprinting is possible for a short time, it shouldn't be taken for granted and it should be noted that at some point it will be necessary to slow down or stop. It is also important to recognize that the cost of working on one thing may mean an opportunity is lost to work on something else. Finishing Project A one month early while Project B pays by being one month late is not cycle-time improvement.

Cycle-Time in Flow Systems

A flow system exists where once "the ball is rolling," it rolls on until completion. The key to measuring and understanding cycle-time is having distinguishable processes. If repetitive activity is considered where the nature and size of the products are very similar, then the process is the set of steps, their sequence, and the standards imposed on the steps and the products. Different processes are distinguished by differences in these items. For nonrepetitive systems like software engineering, the process is defined by attributes. To measure cycle-time, it is also necessary to determine whether attributes are applicable to the project, the process, or the product.

Table 7-2 shows several attributes with their categorization and some example measures. Remember that attribute measures are empirical. In other words, observations of differences in attributes are analyzed against observations of differences in performance (with special cause variation accounted for) to determine appropriate attributes, their measures, and their effect on expectations.

As shown in the example above, process differentiation is clearly shown by the *standard team* definition and the *methodology used* attributes. In general, if the rating scale for any attribute is different, then the process is different.

Cycle-time measures for each process are based on *standard performance*. That is, the cycle-time for a process or the process time standard (PTS) is based on the attribute values corresponding to average performance influence for that attribute (expectation = 1.0).

The general cycle-time formula for flow systems is:

$$\textit{Cycle-Time} = PTS \ * APCTS$$

PTS   *(Process time standard)* (Months per function point): the measured speed of production for 1 channel in a standard process. Determined from productivity measures (e.g., function points per work month (FP/WM)) for all projects using the process under consideration (weighted average—assume that it defines standard pace, otherwise adjusted for pace variation), and from the average channel size expressed in the same terms as the input

TABLE 7-2 Attributes and Example Measures

Attribute	Measure	Expectation		
			Productivity	Quality
Team Experience	0 = None	0	0.65	0.5
	1 = Low	1	0.8	0.7
	2 = Average	2	1.0	1.0
	3 = High	3	1.7	1.4
Standard Team	Channel	The standard team is 1 lead/analyst, 2 programmer/analysts, and 1 tester (4 persons total).		
Number of Standard Teams Assigned	Count	Project A has 6 standard teams assigned.		
			Productivity	Quality
Worker Privacy	0 = Bullpen	0	0.5	0.5
	1 = 4 person/cubicle	1	0.7	0.7
	2 = 4 person/office	2	1.0	1.0
	3 = 2 person/either	3	1.1	1.1
	4 = 1 person/cubicle	4	1.5	1.3
	5 = private office	5	2.0	1.5
Development Platform	a = mainframe	For Productivity: a = 1.0		
	b = mini	b = 1.25		
	c = micro	c = 2.0		
			Productivity	Quality
Total Test Coverage (including inspection)	0 = <30%	0	1.4	0.5
	1 = 30% - 60%	1	1.2	0.7
	2 = 60% - 80%	2	1.0	1.0
	3 = 80% - 95%	3	0.7	1.1
	4 = >95%	4	0.9	1.3
	5 = 100%	5	1.1	2.0
Methodology Used	Name	RAD Waterfall		
			Quality	
Configuration Management (CM)	Yes/No	Yes	1.0	
		No	0.8	
			Productivity	
CM Tools	a = Manual	a	0.8	
	b = Commercial tool	b	0.95	
	c = In-house standard	c	1.0	
	d = Custom	d	?	
			Productivity	Quality
Language	a = 2GL	a	0.8	0.8
	b = 3GL	b	1.0	1.0
	c = 4GL/SS/dB	c	1.5	1.3
			Productivity	Quality
Code Reusability (Reusable Code (Lines)/Total Code (Lines)	1 = none	1	1.4	1.0
	2 = < 30%	2	1.0	1.0
	3 = 30% - 60%	3	0.9	1.0
	4 = 60% - 90%	3	0.8	1.05
	5 = > 90%	4	0.7	1.1
		5	0.5	1.3

side of the productivity measure (e.g., 3-person teams—engineer, programmer, tester) are used such that projects are always staffed in increments of 3. 3WM = 1 channel)

APCTS *(Average per channel task size)*: Size (FP for software projects) for all projects considered in the process time standard in standard size units.

Flow System Cycle-Time Measurement Example

A software development organization has one process and has developed 10 products using this process. A good measurement program is in place and adequate data are available to measure cycle-time. Productivity measures are based on a comprehensive labor charging system. Pace for all projects is 1.0.

The following data are available for these projects:

Project	Size (FP)	# of Channels	Measured Productivity (FP/WM)	Project Productivity Expectation	Duration (Months)
A	1400	3	13.5	0.90	10
B	900	1	19.5	1.30	12
C	750	2	15.0	1.00	7
D	1150	2	18.0	1.20	9
E	800	2	14.3	0.95	7
F	1100	1	15.0	1.00	20
G	1000	2	12.0	0.80	14
H	1350	3	10.5	0.70	12
I	700	1	21.0	1.40	10
J	850	1	15.0	1.00	16

Average project size = 1000 FP
Process Productivity Standard = 15FP/WM

Cycle-Time Example:

$$PTS = \frac{1\,month}{60\,FP} = .016667$$

ATS = 1000 FP

$$Cycle - Time = \frac{.016667\,months}{Fp} * 1000\,FP = 16.7\ months$$

Implication: As processes are improved, the average productivity expectation would increase and the effect of the improvements on cycle time would be reflected in the calculation.

Cycle-Time in Queuing Systems

Queuing systems dominate the maintenance and service arena of software engineering. The customer must wait in line. If the line is long, the length of the wait can be far longer than it takes to perform the service. From the customer's perspective, the length of the wait is important. From the provider's perspective, queue management and the length of time it takes to perform the service are important. Figure 7-5 illustrates a typical queuing system.

The general cycle-time formula for queuing systems (the measure considers observation for a time period) is:

$$Cycle\text{-}Time = \frac{((AAC * NC) + (AADBC * NB))}{(NC + NB) * ANC}$$

AAC *(Average age of completions)*: (number of months) the average age of all items completed during the observation period. The duration of each item should be exclusive of any time for which the work was actually delayed.

NC *(Number of items completed)*: the number of items in the AAC set of completed items.

AABC *(Average age for backlog at completion)*: (number of months) the average for backlog items considering the estimated completion time (date) for each backlog item.

NB *(Number of items in backlog)*: the number of items in the AABC set of backlog items.

ANC *(Average number of channels)*: N

A typical software engineering reaction is that the AABC component is too subjective or not feasible since it requires a realistic estimate of all items that are considered backlog. An alternative method is to take the average age of the backlog at the time of the measurement. This makes the cycle-time result lower, but it is more objective and more sensitive to real improvements in the cycle-time that affect all customers—not just those whose tasks were completed.

Backlog Profiling

In its simplest form, backlog profiling is a graphical representation of a queuing system, with the number of items put into and through the system shown relative to the time at which they were introduced. For example, say

FIGURE 7-5   A Typical Queuing System

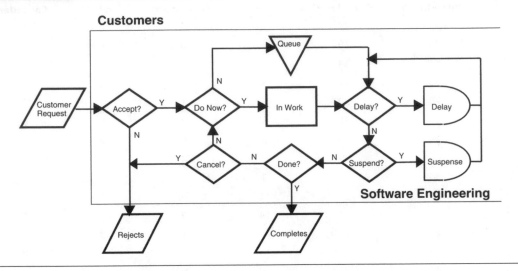

the oldest item in a group or department's backlog is 18 months. A useful profile would track the introduction date of the oldest current backlog item and then list all items introduced during and since that period, indicating the status of those items as completed, in work, delayed, suspended, or cancelled. Backlog profiling is an important process for queuing systems. It is not uncommon for software engineering organizations to have many months or even several years of backlog, with much of the backlog never being introduced into work in process (WIP). It is often politically expedient to have a large backlog even though it may include items that will never be processed.

Table 7-3 shows a postulated set of backlog data and its profile. Figure 7-6 shows a backlog profile for these data.

In Figure 7-6, the work items are displayed in the bottom two series and the average age of WIP and the delay (or queue) are shown. The magnitude of suspensions, rate of cancellations, and average age of completion are also shown, but possibly not quite as obvious. Some simple calculations and redisplaying the order and/or display type for these data make the backlog profile a very useful tool in managing a queuing system. For example, in the data in Figure 7-6, there seems to be a steady trend of a few persistent WIP items that take longer than the apparent average duration of the majority of the items. These items should be reviewed to see if they should be designated as separately managed projects.

Period	Introduced	Completed	In-Work	Suspended	Delayed	Cancelled
-18	35	24	2	3	4	2
-17	23	19	4	0	0	0
-16	41	34	5	0	0	2
-15	33	22	4	2	3	2
-14	28	20	5	1	1	1
-13	37	30	5	2	0	0
-12	54	49	3	0	2	0
-11	44	32	5	4	2	1
-10	38	33	3	1	1	0
-9	47	31	11	0	5	0
-8	31	11	14	2	4	0
-7	29	18	8	1	2	0
-6	38	22	13	0	3	0
-5	42	21	19	0	2	0
-4	40	24	12	1	3	0
-3	34	15	12	0	5	2
-2	43	11	21	1	10	0
-1	37	3	7	2	23	2
Current	29	0	3	0	26	0

TABLE 7-3 Set of Backlog Data

Measuring and managing cycle-time for software engineering presents precisely the same set of problems and issues as it does in manufacturing or other disciplines. The general project orientation of software engineering, along with the general immaturity of measurement as a separate software

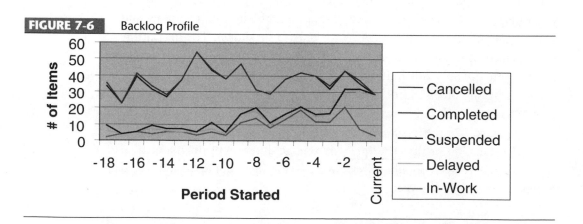

FIGURE 7-6 Backlog Profile

engineering function, is confusing, especially when the goals and objectives of areas where cycle-time is better understood and managed are imposed on software engineering managers and practitioners. Fortunately, in precise measurement terms, it is almost always never too late to do something better.

CHEAPER: THE MEASUREMENT OF PRODUCTIVITY

Productivity measurement is one of the most talked about yet least understood disciplines associated with measurement and managing with metrics. Claims of doubling productivity for new products or methods are often widely proclaimed. Are these claims serious, can they really be believed? At the same time, improving productivity by as little as 10 percent in one year has been labeled "excellent," or "world class" performance.

These types of claims can't both be right, can they? They can if each uses a different definition of productivity. As with many words in the English language, there is more than one correct definition of *productivity*, and each claim is plausible under one of those definitions. If the difference only extended to interpreting hyperbole, what difference would it make? One could just decide which definition was intended and continue on with business. Generally, the confusion goes far beyond that. In reality, many organizations invest considerable time and resources in measurement programs that fail to recognize the two main definitions of productivity, and therefore, miss the opportunity for improvement that effective measurement of productivity can offer. Most literature and available support for measurement do little to improve the position of fledgling practitioners because even experienced personnel collectively seem to miss the distinction.

Many have complained that the application of many measurement and process improvement principles, concepts, and tools is especially difficult in software engineering and in other areas of knowledge work or custom processing because the examples always illustrate repetitive manufacturing. It is easy to analyze a machine operation in widget production. Quality principles are easily understood when discussing sampling widgets in lots with lot size expressed in scientific notation. But, there are no easily understood machines (vendor showcases notwithstanding) for knowledge and custom work. Lot sizes are measured with one finger. The process may be repeated on the next project 18 months later (24 with schedule correction), but it is really not the same because this project is quite different from the previous one.

So, what good are the cures if they are not designed for the specific type of patient? More to the point, what good is it to measure productivity for projects that vary widely or for sporadic processes with long intervals between applications? The answer is not helpful if you intend to use the information for repetitive manufacturing.

To overcome this misunderstanding of how to apply and use productivity measures, it is important to look at what productivity measurement really is. Most people believe that productivity measurement is only the ratio of inputs to a process or activity to its outputs; they are half right. This is the economic productivity definition. This meaning is always used when comparing our national economic productivity with that of other nations or, for example, in software engineering disciplines where productivity measures such as FP/WM are evaluated.

But, if one really wants to effectively use the tool productivity measurement, its other definition—the ratio of an expected value to an actual or observed value—must be considered. This is often seen, for example, when there is a claim that a particular tool will improve productivity by a phenomenal amount. In reality, this claim means that for the task for which the tool is used, it will offer a 50 percent improvement in the performance of that task over the performance expected without that tool. How much that means to the bottom line depends on the amount of the bottom line that the original task affected. It is only through the concept of expected value that it is possible to go beyond the mere quantification of productivity to actually developing a clear understanding of the productivity of an activity and then use that understanding to evaluate and control the productivity of processes.

There are two groups of people in the world: those who divide everything into two groups and those who don't. Similarly, there are two groups of causation that determine the performance of any process or activity: common causes and special causes. *Common causes*, as their name implies, apply a process from each incident to the next incident. The influence of a common cause on the outcome of instance "A" of a process is the same or essentially the same as its influence on instance "N" of the same process. In other words, doing the same thing over and over will give the same results over and over (barring special cause, which is discussed later).

From this principle, it is possible to see the logic of using control charts. Numerous things other than real changes in what is being measured will cause measures to vary. Based on the principle that common causes will exert the same influence on future performance as was exerted in the past, the history of process performance can predict current and future performance. Given natural variation in both the process and its measurement, it is possible to establish a mean past performance and an interval around that mean within which any process can be expected to perform. The degree of confidence is usually expressed as a percentage value based on how the interval is determined. For example, a process with normally distributed common cause variation would use a control range of ± 3 standard deviations and state its associated 97 percent confidence that any measured performance occurring within that range is due to common causes of variation. It is important to remember that understanding the past influence of common causes on performance allows prediction of their future influence on performance. Figure 7-7 illustrates how a process behaves over time.

Another important point associated with common causes of variation is that the statistical process control method only measures the influence of the common causes without identifying what they actually are and without evaluating their influence beyond the context of actual level of influence and association with the other common causes influencing the same performance.

The basis of successful productivity measurement rests on the concept that each common cause of performance can be evaluated in terms of its particular influence on performance as to its own level of use and the context within which it is used. Further, this information can accurately predict future performance of an activity without precise knowledge of that activity's historical performance, but with knowledge of the common causes that will influence that activity's performance.

The implications of this ability to accurately predict untested activities are the judicious selection of an activity's common causes to engineer the

FIGURE 7-7   Control Chart Example

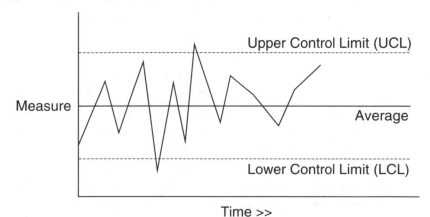

performance result for that activity before it is undertaken. This level of performance control implies tremendous opportunity for improvement in performance and the reduction of risk associated with unpredictability for an activity.

IMPROVEMENT OF PROCESSES

Finally, measurement is pure cost, and unless information is used to improve process, it is mostly wasted. To paraphrase Dr. Deming, process improvement is not something to talk about, it is something to do.[1] Much more is said than done when discussing process improvement in complex and variable processes. What is worse, far too much of what is done is performed incorrectly—the process is not better and process improvement itself is tainted. Let's look at process improvement and determine if there is a way to effectively and consistently improve complex processes.

Two things need to be understood: process and improvement. The numerous different definitions and their imprecision have resulted in confusion and misunderstanding about process improvement. The operating definition of process is: *the way in which something is intended to be done.* Any process has an accomplishment objective. A process must describe the steps for achieving its objective as well as the means for performing the steps. Because this is a very general definition, it is assumed that for complex processes, our process has a formal definition such that it can be nearly repeated. Therefore, a prerequisite for process improvement is that there must be a comprehensive process definition.

Now, contrast process with project. A process is the intended method, whereas a project is the application of resources to that process. Since projects are tangible, the only way a process can be measured is to measure the projects and use the information to make inferences about the process. As a measurement tool, process is the category to which common causes of variation are assigned. Projects are affected by both common and special causes of variation. Working on special causes is problem identification and correction, whereas working on common causes is process improvement. To go one step further, using special cause tools and methods on common causes and vice-versa is called *meddling.* Meddling invariably causes "fires," and fire-fighting does not improve processes.

Three characteristics describe any process. *Efficiency (E)* is the relationship comparing the use of resources to accomplished results. *Cycle-time (T)* is the design speed of the process. Finally, every process has a *quality (Q)* characteristic. When someone says, "good, fast, cheap—pick two," this is more insight than humor. For any process, there is a function (F). This function embodies the three characteristics of efficiency, cycle-time, and quality. Therefore:

$$F(E,T,Q) = \text{Constant K}$$

For better, and faster, *and* cheaper, you need a different process.

Sequence and means are the two elements of a process. *Sequence* is the order in which things are done. There are two types of sequence: required (precedence) and discretionary. *Required sequence* is an order that must be followed. Project managers should be familiar with this concept from the program evaluation review technique (PERT) methodology. For example, a prerequisite for a second coat of paint is that the first coat has already been applied and cured. In software development, it is best to start coding after the requirements are gathered. *Discretionary sequence* is the order in which it is decided that something will be done. The required sequence must be observed. In practice, precedence and resource availability control the process execution sequence decision.

After sequence is completed, the means by which the steps or tasks will be carried out are determined. This aspect is sometimes referred to as the application of resources to a process to produce a result. Resources are labor, plant and equipment, and time and money; however, to understand the process, other resources must be considered, such as tools, techniques, and technology, as well as factors particular to resources such as the team members' skills and experience. Therefore, all aspects must be considered to understand and improve processes. It is helpful to consider the means in categories such as management, technology, teams (or people), tools, techniques, and environment.

An organization must consider all its processes collectively when considering improvement. Thus, a process has been described as a sequence and a set of means. By this definition, each organization would have an infinite number of processes (possible combinations of E, T, and Q). This introduces two more dimensions of process: *capability* and *capacity*.

Each possible combination of E, Q, and T defines a capability. The current ability of an organization to execute a capability defines capacity. This is not as complicated as it appears. For example, one of the means defined as "Red" team is comprised of members with certain experience and knowledge. Red team projects are done faster, better, and cheaper than "Blue" or "Green" team projects. Red team performance levels are a capability. However, the number of employees qualified to be designated for the Red team is limited within the organization; therefore, there is a capacity associated with Red team capability.

There are two categories of improvement: continuous improvement and innovation. *Continuous improvement* of processes is systematic upgrading to yield higher capacity at a higher capability. To use the previous example, continuous improvement of team capability would provide training to Blue and Green team members so that more Red teams could be formed. *Innovation* is the introduction of new capability. For example, innovation would be training everyone—all teams—in a new technique. Everyone, even the Red team, would have a greater capability to execute the new technique.

The distinction between the two types of improvement is not clear-cut. The important point for organizations to remember is that innovation usually introduces learning curve dynamics and a risk of failure to a greater extent than continuous improvement.

It is necessary to make another distinction between strategy and process improvement. Again using the team example, if a strategy were pursued to lay off Green and Blue team members and replace them with Red team-qualified candidates at similar cost, better values of performance (E, Q, and T) would be expected. In reality, Red team-caliber candidates have higher salaries and are much harder to find. On the other hand, effective process improvement requires understanding the process. It is necessary to know what will actually improve a process and the amount it will improve. First, it is necessary to figure out the cost of making Blue and Green team members perform like the Red team; next, the benefit of improving team performance must be computed.

When dealing with complexity, what is obvious is not always true and what is true is not always obvious. Improving understanding of the process is the only way to manage the risk that changes will not result in the desired improvement.

There are still two categories of process that need to be considered in applying the process improvement tools available. There are *repetitive processes*, like most manufacturing and some construction, and there are *nonrepetitive processes*, like software engineering. The definition is not *a priori*, that is, it is impossible to specify up-front what the particular process is. However, if understanding is not achieved when trying to apply the tools for understanding a repetitive process, then you must classify the process as nonrepetitive and use the tools having a higher capability for understanding complex processes.

Repetitive Processes

In process improvement literature, there is much available information to support repetitive process improvement. Virtually all the common process and statistical process control (SPC) literature focuses on repetitive process principles and examples. Characteristics of these processes are a mostly fixed precedence: sequence and means (what is done, when it is done, and how it is done). Generally, the process flow chart tool is used to understand and improve these processes. Care is taken to use the decision element of this tool to divide flow into segments that are distributed so that SPC tools can analyze the data. (Refer back to Table 7-1 for the flow chart tool symbols and concepts used to analyze repetitive processes.)

Nonrepetitive Processes

For nonrepetitive processes, attempts to understand and improve using repetitive process tools and techniques yield the same results as trying to teach pigs to sing: there is no singing and the pigs are upset. The key to understanding nonrepetitive processes is that even though the steps and sequence are never the same from project to project, the means generally are. That is, in most cases, the same teams (individuals and skills) with the same management (individuals, styles, and leadership), using the same tools and techniques in the same environment will work on a different project. In any case, there are myriad things about the means (management, teams, tools, techniques, environment, etc.) that can be measured so that variation in these measures can be related to variations in performance (E, T, and Q) for any project.

Looking at the process flow chart tool description (Table 7-1), the volume property of the arrows along with the normalization use of decisions allow an analyst to normalize out variation due to throughput and size. For nonrepetitive processes, project cost, defects, and duration will vary not only from differences in the means of accomplishing completion, but also due to the size.

The reason size measurement hasn't been mentioned previously is that it seems to work like a light switch. Flip the switch, and about half the people turn on like a light, and the others turn off. The goal of a size measure is to get variation due to size out of the analysis without introducing another source of variation or removing a process-related source of performance variation. If the size measure accomplishes this—straightforward statistical analysis will indicate this—then you are on the right track.

Size measures are not an explicit consideration in all types of projects. In cases where the projects' sizes are similar enough to ensure that variation due to size is not a major factor or where differences in size are tangible and clearly related to their effects, it is not a problem that is posed to the project manager. Where differences in size are significant and the measures of size are not clearly tangible or easily determined such as in systems, software, or service projects, measurement fails through an inability to determine or agree on the size of the project (ratio measure) or the relationship of the size of one project to another (interval measure).

In conclusion, there is improvement in nonrepetitive processes. Understanding of these processes comes from analyzing the effects of variation in the means of production on performance. To illustrate how this translates into reality, let's use the example of the Software Engineering Institute (SEI) Capability Maturity Model (CMM®). The SEI CMM® measures process capability maturity on a scale of 1 to 5, with 5 being more mature. Several practitioners and analysts have also developed relationships between the SEI CMM® maturity level and performance in each dimension of process measurement (E, T, and Q). Notably, the higher the maturity level, the better the performance. Based on available analyses, the differences are substantial and one assumes that they are statistically significant.

The nonrepetitive process improvement model is analogous to this view of the SEI CMM®. That is, for each of the means (management, teams, tools, techniques, environment, etc.), a scale of possible conditions is developed and criteria are prepared for evaluating that means according to that scale. For example, project management is the means being evaluated. The low end of the scale would be no project management, maybe a lead, and no formal tracking. The top of the scale would be a full-time project manager reporting to the project management office and using a full set of project management (e.g., PMI's PMBOK®) tools. With all means identified and a scale created for each of the means, the values of the means for any given project constitute a process.

Improvement of the process is really the improvement of the means. Figure 7-8 shows how a process is managed to obtain a performance result. For the organization measured, the scale in each means (e.g., management) represents the range of influence of the measured capability measured on performance. For any project, the actual value of the mean (the triangle symbol) predicts the contribution of that aspect to the overall project performance. The process model shows the collective effect of the measured means values on project performance and gives the project predicted performance.

FIGURE 7-8   Management of a Process to Obtain a Performance Result

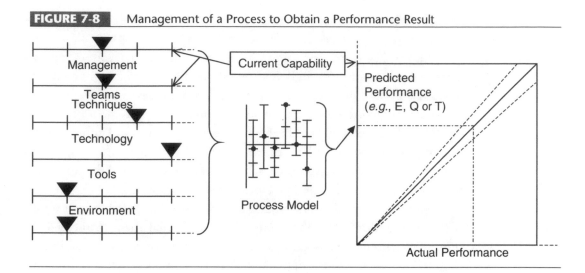

The goal of performance measurement then becomes measuring actual performance against predicted performance to detect problems. Process improvement is working on the means, both for capability (higher levels on the scale) and for capacity (how much is available for use).

Project management is:

1. Identifying the process used (and predicted performance)
2. Ensuring that the actual performance equals predicted performance.

Process improvement is:

1. Improving capacity at each higher level of capability
2. Increasing your capability in each of the process areas.

If you know what you are doing, calibrating the model is straightforward. That is, for any given set of means, values for E, Q, and T (exclusive of special causes) can be predicted. Therefore, if the model is calibrated, the effect of changes in the means (benefits) can also be quantified. Finally, understanding the means makes the actions and investments necessary to move up the scale evident and their cost (time and money) easily determined. Now the action, cost, and benefit of process improvement can be analyzed objectively. Finally, "more can be done than said."

It is important to note that even in a calibrated model it is likely that the variation in performance effect for the lower levels of a means is much greater than for higher levels. That translates into the risk that the prediction at low levels will be off. In analysis, these are prediction anomalies called outliers and are ignored. In reality, they must be accommodated. Compare this with SEI CMM® Level 1 stellar performers —at Level 1, the model is not predictive. However, the overwhelming odds are that Level 1 performance will be worse than the performance at higher levels.

The real key to process improvement is to know what you are doing. There is nothing intuitive in doing something that makes its improvement obvious ("perfect practice makes perfect"). For process improvement to succeed, it is the project team's skill level in process improvement that must be high and not the skill level in the process being improved. Unfortunately, most organizations do not have the requisite skills among their management or staff. No matter how motivated, facilitated, or well-directed the team is, a team needs the right skills to implement process improvement.

In a typical organization, process improvement has failed at least once. If the team is blamed, it was wrong to have expected them to succeed. If process improvement was blamed, that was also incorrect—it is alive and well, and works great in the right hands. The right resources must be brought together in the right place at the right time with the right management and right leadership.

What will your measurement program include? To succeed, it needs to include all necessary components. Encourage customers to make it do so. How good is the measurement program going to be? Every bit as good as it is possible to make it. Strive and encourage others to make it so. Use the measurement program to inspire and inform the thought process, while avoiding the temptation to let the results of measurement replace thinking. Quality is better, things go faster, and cost is lower—not because the measures say these things are true. They are true because causes can be cited that may have affected these results and then the measures can be used to validate the related changes in results. Remember what was said about insanity—doing the same things and expecting different results. It must also be citing different results without being able to identify that things have changed.

So, go forth and multiply, and add, subtract, divide, infer, differentiate, hypothecate—and above all—make it work.

NOTE

1. W. E. Deming, *Out of the Crisis* (Cambridge, MA: MIT Center for Advanced Engineering Study, 1986).

CHAPTER 8

Wrap-up and Key Points

The material in this book should help you achieve success in measurement. Measurement is a separate discipline from what is being measured. Simply knowing or understanding a process thoroughly so that changes in results can be traced to their causes, or recognizing the impact of those changes, is not the same as knowing how to measure that process. Nor does it lay the groundwork for conceiving and implementing a measurement program that will meet the goals inspired by the measurement program. For measurement to be effective and to succeed, stakeholder requirements must be reflected in the structure and operation of the measurement program.

IT'S A MOVING TARGET

Since measurement supports the evolution of the subject being measured, measurement must evolve also. If we expect rapid change, then it follows that measurement supporting the change decisions and validating the change results must evolve as fast, if not faster, than the change itself. Measurement has a definite lifecycle. A generic learning cycle applies to measurement where the discipline or process being examined is not measured and is not particularly effective, efficient, or robust.

The first step in the maturing process is to change the awareness of the process itself through measurement and quantitative tools. At the high end, where changes to the process are small and infrequent, the need for measurement decreases and the process evolves to a state of being efficient, effective, and robust without the need for measurement to confirm this state (unconscious competence). Cost savings are important because measurement can be costly.

SOME MYTHS AND FACTS ABOUT MEASUREMENT

Myth: Measurement is expensive. *Fact:* Measurement is a cost.

Myth: Measurements can be used against the persons being measured. *Fact:* The myth is true in the same sense that matches can be used to incinerate civilization.

Myth: Measuring improves processes. ***Fact:*** Processes can be improved only by changing the processes.

Myth: It won't work here. ***Fact:*** Whether it seems possible or not, it is probably a correct assessment.

Measurement works on the bottom line by enabling process proficiency and/or improvement. An effective measurement program will identify all the facets necessary for success as it works toward evaluating the alignment of these facets. Measurement is beneficial. However, measurement is deceptively simple-looking, and a misguided venture into measurement can easily create more problems than it solves.

What are measures? Analogous to the hierarchy of data → information → knowledge → wisdom, measures are the data of a measurement program.

What are metrics? Continuing with the hierarchy view, metrics are the information dimension of measurement.

TYPES OF MEASURES

There are numerous types of measures:

- Nominal measures define categories and relationships.
- Ordinal measures define relative relationships.
- Interval measures quantify relative relationships.
- Ratio measures define absolute values.
- Characterization of metrics is done by purpose.
- Efficiency measures tell that things are done correctly.
- Effectiveness measures tell that individuals are doing the right things.
- Health measures tell how well individuals are able to continue to do the right things correctly.

Too often, efficiency measures overshadow effectiveness measures. Success on a project has marginal value if the entire team leaves after the project. This scenario would constitute a poor health measure.

BUILDING BLOCKS FOR A SUCCESSFUL MEASUREMENT PROGRAM

Only a complete program will give complete satisfactory results. The following are measurement critical success factors:

- Accurate
- Timely
- Objective and comprehensible

- Focused on strategic control points
- Economically realistic
- Organizationally realistic
- Coordinated with work flow
- Flexible
- Prescriptive and operational
- Acceptable.

Ensuring that your measurement program meets all these factors is critical to its success.

ONE SIZE DOES NOT FIT ALL

In reality, at least three measurement programs need to be in place for measurement to succeed:

1. At an executive or strategic level
2. At a management or tactical level
3. At a task or technical level.

STAKEHOLDER ANALYSIS

The primary purpose of measurement is to communicate. Therefore, it is vitally important to identify what is being communicated, to whom it is being communicated, and how it is being communicated. Stakeholder analysis is a method to ensure that the communication requirements are met and that waste associated with measuring and communicating information for which there is no identified customer is eliminated.

IMPLEMENTING A MEASUREMENT PROGRAM

Measurement is a tool that the enterprise must use to evaluate its performance thoroughly and objectively and to identify improvement opportunity. The enterprise leaders must provide the measurement tools and must, if necessary, insist on their use. Do not be surprised if those who would benefit most from an effective measurement system are its biggest opponents. Managing people and managing change present much greater challenges than does the measurement itself.

The following four categorizations (in order of resolution) describe the challenges to a successful metrics program:

1. People issues
2. Commitment issues
3. Process issues
4. Measurement issues.

If the issues raised are correctly classified and managed, there is an excellent chance of success.

IT'S IN THE PLANNING

Implementing measurement is a project. The key to success for any project is planning. However, having the measurement in place is not the real objective of the measurement project; it is having the measurement used by the organization. If after measurement is implemented, decisions are still made the old way without significant use of the data, then interest and support for the measurement will quickly drop off. Tools make the impossible possible; they make the difficult easier. The performance index matrix (PIM) is a tool that keeps the organization focused on the goals and not on the details.

MATURING THE MEASUREMENT PROGRAM

Measurement is a powerful tool. It is reasonable to expect that as the measurement program matures, routine measurement will decrease to a level of monitoring types of measurements and exception reporting. Responsiveness to special requests is important to maintaining the resources necessary to champion the measurement program as it and the organization evolve, especially since it is certain that there will be continuing challenges to measurement.

After all, measurement is still a game of chance. But the way one plays the game greatly increases the odds of success even against formidable obstacles.

Bibliography

Deming, W. E. *Out of the Crisis* (Cambridge, MA: MIT Center for Advanced Engineering Study, 1986).

Drucker, P. *Management: Tasks, Responsibilities, Practices* (New York: Harper & Row, 1974).

Goldratt, E., and J. Cox. *The Goal: A Process of Ongoing Improvement* (Great Barrington, MA: North River Press, 1985).

Senge, P. *The Fifth Discipline: The Art and Practice of the Learning Organization* (New York: Currency/Doubleday, 1994).

Stoner, J.A. *Management* (Englewood Cliffs, NJ: Prentice-Hall, 1978).

Verdugo, Gonzalo G. "Measurement Program Design: Addressing the Needs of Project and Application Support Teams," Rubin and Associates, Presentation to Quality Assurance Institute Ninth International Conference, March 20-21, 1991.

Index